Helping
Children
Grieve

Helping Children Grieve

When Someone They Love Dies

Theresa Huntley

Augsburg • Minneapolis

HELPING CHILDREN GRIEVE
When Someone They Love Dies

Scripture quotations unless otherwise noted are from the Holy Bible: New International Version. Copyright 1978 by the New York International Bible Society. Used by permission of Zondervan Bible Publishers.

Cover design: Steve Diggs & Friends

Library of Congress Cataloging-in-Publication Data

Huntley, Theresa, 1961–
    Helping children grieve : when someone they love dies / Theresa Huntley.
       p. cm.
    ISBN 0-8066-2549-X
    1. Children and death. 2. Grief in children. 3. Bereavement in children. 4. Children—Counseling of. I. Title.
    BF723.D3H86   1991
    155.9'37—dc20   91-12631
                                                                    CIP

The paper used in this publication meets the minimum requirements of American National Standard for Information Sciences—Permanence of Paper for Printed Library Materials, ANSI Z329.48-1984. ∞™

Manufactured in the U.S.A.   AF 9-2549

14   15

Contents

To Molly,
a special friend,
whose courage and strength
have been a source
of great inspiration
in my life.

Introduction

Y OU HAVE JUST RECEIVED a tragic phone call. Your wife has been killed in an auto accident. It seems too terrible to even think about, and yet you have two children at the sitter's who must be told of their mother's death. How do you even begin to approach the discussion?

Your father's last heart attack caused great damage and his doctor says he will live only a few months more. Your three-year-old child is asking lots of questions. She is very close to her grandfather and doesn't understand what is happening to him. Now you are wondering: "Should I try to explain what it means to be so sick that the body can't work right and eventually quits working altogether? Or should I protect my child from the painful reality of death and simply say, 'Grandpa is going away on a long trip and may not be able to visit anymore'? At least that way she could look forward to the possibility of a visit from her grandfather at some point in the future. I know he won't be visiting, but she doesn't. Maybe she'd adjust better if she didn't know."

You are a teacher. A student in your class has recently been diagnosed with cancer, and he will soon be coming back to school. He's been away for several weeks, and you haven't specifically told his classmates what has been happening to him. Now you are wondering: "Do I accept the offer from the hospital nurse who said she'd make a presentation to the class about cancer? Or do I just say nothing? Are the children even old enough to understand the information? After all, they *are* only six years old. Maybe it would be better to wait and see how things go."

Your child has been watching the movie *Bambi*. She is very distressed when the mother doesn't come back after a romp with Bambi in the meadow. Do you take this opportunity to introduce the topic of death? Or do you create a story about where the mother has gone for the remainder of the show? After all, it is only a story. What could it hurt to let your child think that it all works out OK?

The words *children* and *death* seem to contradict one another. When we think of death, we often think simultaneously of old age. We certainly don't think of children! And yet, as we know, death happens, and not just to old people. It is a reality of life faced by everyone, regardless of age.

As much as we might want to protect children from death, we simply cannot. Whether we discuss it with them or not, children are aware of death. If we give them the message that it is not OK to talk about it, they will take their questions to someone else.

Rather than attempting to hide death from children, we need to help them explore the concept in a safe, nonthreatening manner. Ideally, they will learn to think of death more often as a natural part of life, and less often as a frightening occurrence to be dreaded.

Teaching children about death is not an easy task. Many people choose not to instruct children about the concept. They assume that if children don't talk about it, they're not thinking about it. Anyone reading this book, however, probably realizes this is not true. You are willing to face the challenge of teaching your children about death and are seeking information that will assist you.

This book is intended for everyone who spends any amount of time with children. We know that children are inquisitive. They seem to have a never-ending flow of questions about the world and everything in it. They also wonder about death. My purpose in writing this book is to help increase your awareness of how children understand and experience death. To protect the identities of the children and their families, I have changed the names and altered some of the circumstances in each story. The book can be read from beginning to end, or you can choose those chapters that are appropriate for your situation. It is our responsibility to prepare our children for the inevitable losses of life and to help them grieve when those times come.

1

How Infants and Preschoolers Understand Death

W HEN TALKING WITH CHILDREN ABOUT DEATH, it is helpful to understand how children view death at different stages of their lives. We all know that a three-year-old comprehends things differently than a twelve-year-old. But we are not always sure what that difference is. Without this information, it is difficult to know how to approach a subject like death.

Death is certainly not an easy concept to understand, but we want children to at least develop a healthy, objective attitude toward it. So, we must be aware of how children of different ages understand death and tailor death education to their specific needs.

Children gradually develop a concept of death directly related to their age. Of course, children's understanding of death is affected by other factors, including psychological development, emotional maturity, coping abilities, previous experiences in life, environment, culture, and parental attitudes. For now, the discussion will focus on the child's understanding of death only as it relates to age.

Specific patterns of thinking and behaving are unique to children at different stages in their development. Although many of these characteristics overlap, we can look at those stages as five distinct groups based on levels of development: 1) Children less than three years old (infancy and toddlerhood); 2) Three- to six-year-olds (preschool); 3) Six- to ten-year-olds (early school-age); 4) Ten- to twelve-year-olds (early adolescence); and 5) Twelve- to eighteen-year-olds (adolescence).

9

These groups are approximations and should be used only as guides. Each child is an individual, and his or her understanding of death will be affected by multiple factors as previously mentioned. Each child's situation must be recognized as unique and assessed accordingly.

Children Less Than Three Years of Age; Infancy and Toddlerhood

Children in this first age group do not understand the concept of death. Infants and toddlers depend heavily on their parents. As a result, they worry most about separation, particularly from their mothers. For them, dying means separation.

Infants

Infants have the task of differentiating themselves from the environment. A. Maurer, quoted in *Listening and Responding*, maintains that in order to develop a sense of being, infants also develop a sense of nonbeing.[1]

In *Explaining Death to Children*, Robert Kastenbaum suggests that certain experiences and behaviors of very young children imply a relationship to the state of nonbeing.[2] For example, as infants alternate between the state of sleeping and the state of wakefulness, they may gain a basic appreciation of the difference between being and nonbeing.

By approximately three months of age, healthy infants are secure enough to begin experimenting through games with the contrasting states of being and nonbeing. The first example of this is the game *peek-a-boo*. It provides a safe opportunity for infants to experience both fear and delight. At first the baby responds with wide eyes when the blanket is removed. Then delighted coos follow when the child makes eye contact with a smiling face.

Toddlers

During the high-chair age, infants and toddlers play games of *disappear and return*, in which they drop toys or other objects from their trays and wait for someone to retrieve them. Children delight to see the objects reappear and will repeat the activity over and over again. Gradually, however, they suspect that not all things return; they are *all gone*. This, then, becomes a favorite phrase.

Once children begin to appreciate *all-goneness*, they will continue to experiment with being and nonbeing through game-playing with all-gone situations. These situations will produce curiosity and sometimes even fear.

For example, Lance, a toddler who is being toilet trained, becomes proud of himself when he is able to poop in the toilet. He might, however, consider his feces to be a part of his body; seeing it being flushed away could prompt him to try to retrieve what is his.

The drain in the bathtub is another example of experimenting with all-goneness. Toddlers are fascinated by the water swirling around the drain after the plug has been pulled. But they are quick to get out of the tub before they too are all gone.

Blowing out a lighted match, turning a light switch off and on, and flushing toys down the toilet (only to have them retrieved by a plumber) are also experiments with being and nonbeing. These experiments are some of the child's earliest representations of the expression of self.

Children Three to Six Years of Age; Preschool

Children in the next age group, three- to six-year-olds, view the world from the perspective of their own experiences. Megan was three when her great-grandfather died. Despite the fact that her parents prepared her for the wake, the funeral, and the burial, Megan's questions and responses indicated that she didn't really understand. She was heard to say, "Shhh. We have to be quiet 'cause he's sleeping." "Why isn't he moving?" "Will I be dead too?" "Will you be dead?" "How will he breathe?" "Can he eat?" Her parents responded honestly and simply to Megan's questions, and with time her understanding increased.

Although children at this age may use the words *die* and *dead*, they cannot truly comprehend what they have not yet experienced. Their vocabularies, although increasing, are also limited. Consequently, preschoolers rely on what they have learned from adults, peers, books read to them, and television. They imitate those around them and experiment with words.

At approximately age three or four, children begin to discuss death and to think about it in their own simple way. The discussion is somewhat limited because they do not yet understand the concept. They do, however, think about it enough to arouse negative feelings.

Even young children seem to recognize that death is something unique, although they cannot comprehend exactly what makes it so. Children as young as five show more emotional reaction to words related to death than to other types of words.[3]

Young children understand the day-to-day things in life and the feelings of their families who take care of them. During this early phase in their development, children seem to regard death mainly as separation, a departure. It is clear that the dead are not here with us. For preschoolers, this is probably the most important fact of death.[4] Any separation, or prospect of separation (especially from a parent), is likely to arouse thoughts of death.

The most painful aspect of death for young children, then, is the separation itself, particularly since they may not always differentiate between a short absence and a long or permanent one. It is helpful, therefore, to tell children, in terms they can understand, when we will be returning. For example, when you leave, you might say, "Daddy will be home after lunch," or "We will be at a meeting while you are taking your nap, but we'll be home before supper." By doing this, you will help children become gradually aware of, and comfortable with, the little separations that are a part of everyday life.

Kastenbaum says there is general agreement that young children begin with a matter-of-fact orientation toward death. Their cool or detached inquiry into the subject is accompanied by two important assumptions.

First, they seem to believe that death is accidental, rather than inevitable. A person dies only under certain conditions, and these conditions may or may not occur.

Second, preschoolers assume that they themselves will not die. If they can avoid the conditions, then they can escape death. For example, Ashley is aware that her father died in a car accident. Her thinking is that if she avoids riding in a car, she will avoid the possibility of an accident. Thus, she, unlike her father, will escape the condition of death.

Three- to six-year-olds also believe that death is reversible. Dan Schaefer and Christine Lyons, in *How Do We Tell the Children*, suggest that in order to understand the finality of death, children have to recognize that they are separate from their parents and that without them, they could still exist.[5] Preschoolers cannot do this.

Preschoolers are dependent and know they need protection. A world without their parents is beyond imagination. Thus, young children regard death as temporary. Adults may tell them that death is permanent, a one-way street, but this is difficult to understand. So, preschoolers may continue to think in terms of temporary death, perhaps keeping their thoughts to themselves.

While those in authority contradict the preschoolers' view of death, the media reinforce it. When young children watch animated cartoons, they are constantly confronted with life-unto-death-unto-life dynamics. They see characters on television who die on one show, only to reappear on another, again reinforcing their belief in the reversibility of death.

Preschoolers cannot imagine what it's like to die. They recognize that periodically one's condition changes. In somewhat the same way as you sleep and wake, so too are you made dead, and then return to ordinary life. Even while dead, you still live, although perhaps on a reduced level as while asleep. Consequently, the body functions continue (breathing, eating, urinating, sleeping).

This belief comes through in the questions children ask. Preschoolers want to know such things as: How can the person breathe when we are burying him in the ground? How is he going to get food and drink? Where will he go to the bathroom? How will he see in the dark?

Children this age, when attempting to identify what is alive, depend on the structure and appearance of an object. If something is able to move or can be used, then it is thought to be alive.[6]

Magical thinking and fantasy reasoning are also characteristic of this age group. Young children are convinced of the power of their wishes. They believe, for example, that they can will a person to death or back to life. Most children, at some point, scream, "I hate you! I wish you were dead!" or "I wish you would go away!" When the person does go away forever, or die, children may believe their words or wishes caused it to happen.

Preschoolers are often prone to think superficial or even irrelevant details are involved in death. Becoming increasingly aware that death is something important and destructive, they seek to find those phenomena that mean or cause death.[7]

When asked what causes things to die, preschoolers frequently mention behaviors like not heeding the instructions of their parents. They see the act, rather than the consequences of the act, as the cause of death.[8] For example, if a child runs out into the street without looking first and is struck and killed by a car, she will die—not because she is injured but because she did not look both ways as she had been instructed.

Young children may also take the admonitions of adults quite literally. Sometimes in a moment of exasperation a parent may say, "Honestly! You'll be the death of me yet!" If that parent then dies, the child may think he or she is responsible for the death.

Preschoolers tend to connect events that do not belong together. They lack the reasoning power of adults and seek a beginning, middle, and end to a story. If they are missing facts, they will fill in the blanks from their imaginations.[9]

For example, if a child was wearing a blue jacket when she last saw her grandpa before his death, she might feel her blue jacket caused his death. She may fill in her own "facts" if she is not told the real cause of death: Grandpa's heart attack.

Children this age often see illness or death as punishment for their bad thoughts or actions. For example, if Katie had a fight with her brother and he is killed that afternoon in a car accident, she might think it happened because of the fight. If children accept the guilt, they tend to become passive and withdrawn. If they deny guilt and project it onto others, they may become angry and rebellious.[10]

Death may also be associated with darkness, violence, evil, and sleeping. The world of death is confusing and filled with changes. When things such as sewers, ditches, and boogeymen become a part of the preschooler's thinking, nightmares and a fear of the dark are common.[11]

Finally, preschoolers express less death anxiety than children in other age groups.[12] Yet, they are as sensitive as older children to our nonverbal attitudes. If we are reserved, fearful, paranoid, or hostile, very often children will pick up on these feelings and act just as we do. If we are open, honest, warm, and loving, then they will get the message that this is the way to be.[13]

2

How School-age Children Understand Death

B Y THE TIME A CHILD reaches school age, many changes in thinking have occurred. These are the years of questioning.

Children Six to Ten Years of Age; Early School Age

Children in the six- to ten-year-old age group gradually accept the idea that death is final, inevitable, universal, and personal. Many six- and seven-year-olds suspect their parents will die some day and that the same fate *might* await them. They may accept the facts that someone died and death is final, but they do not yet fully understand that death *must* happen to everyone, including themselves.

Young school-age children may become more secretive than preschoolers, keeping their thoughts and feelings to themselves. They may also speak of death less often and seem uninterested in the concept. After the first premonitions of death, children may delay full recognition of the subject for several years. Perhaps children are still too vulnerable emotionally to accept the implications of their own new thoughts about death. Or perhaps their thoughts are primarily attuned to mastering the realities of daily life.

Whatever the case, it seems that in mid childhood children can neither deny nor accept death in their own lives. Some type of compromise becomes necessary. This might involve an acknowledgement that death is real, but real in an external and distant sense.[1]

At this age, children attribute life to anything capable of spontaneous movement. They are able to differentiate between animate and inanimate objects but continue to believe that the clouds, wind, stars, sun, and rivers are alive.[2]

Although these children are better able to test reality, magical thinking persists. Younger school-age children, like preschoolers, may overestimate the power of their wishes. More significant, however, is the strong tendency to personify death. Children see death as a taker, something evil and violent that will come and get you and stop your life.

Death may also be associated with ghosts, witches, monsters, burglars, or boogeymen. Thus, upon hearing of a death, a child will likely ask, "Who killed him?" In a sense, these death personifications protect children in their belief that only people the death-man catches and carries off will die. Whoever can get away will live.

During the early school-age period, mutilation anxiety, the fear of bodily injury, often becomes a predominant fear. Death becomes frightening and dangerous because children worry that some type of scary being will come and take them away.

Reacting to this anxiety, boys, especially, seek detailed information about death and bodies. Children try to gain a sense of control through their own rational analysis of the situation. They also use fantasy life to confront death. Death is often play-acted in war and violence, and playmates discuss the gory details with one another.

At this age children begin to develop their own sense of moral judgment. They may try to reason out the meaning of life, heaven, and life after death. They also continue to associate death with the fear of retaliation or getting even for wrongdoing. Thus, children may spend much time thinking and worrying about who God is and what God will do to them.

Young school-age children may worry about being abandoned. Fears of separation, although less pronounced than fears of mutilation, continue. Children may even fear that death is contagious. Death anxiety is greatest during this period.[3]

Children Ten to Twelve Years of Age; Early Adolescence

Ten- to twelve-year-olds continue to develop an acute sense of right and wrong. Many still think of death as a punishment for misdeeds.

Although they are making the transition to a more adult concept of death, they may still manifest remnants of magical thinking and the "*I* did it" syndrome.

Somewhere between the ages of nine and twelve, children change from thinking everything that moves is alive to concluding that some things that move are not alive (the sun, stars, and wind). They now understand that the term alive is limited to plants and animals.[4]

It is difficult for children to develop a general concept of death until they have had enough experience with the world to learn what is and is not alive. Early adolescents can better distinguish between animate and inanimate objects. By age ten, if not before, most children hold a nearly adult view of living and not living.[5]

Early adolescents are learning to understand both the biological process of death and the emotional aspects of it. At this point they are better able to understand the *facts* surrounding the death of someone than they are the *feelings*. They may likely have more interest in the biological details of what happened. Unlike younger children, they now have a frame of reference and can handle much of the same information given to an adult.

Death can now be understood in relation to the laws of nature. Early adolescents may generally recognize that death is not an external power that comes upon them, but an internal dysfunction that causes life to end. When asked what causes death, these children will list illness, old age, and accidents, or simply that part of the body no longer works right.[6]

After children reach age twelve, death is seldom, if ever, pictured as a person. Instead, it is visualized as darkness, and it is associated with sadness and evil. At this age, children view death as terrible, horrible, and surrounded by gloom.[7]

Because these children are experimenting with ideas and theories, they may think that death is a way of getting rid of people to make room for new ones. Or they may believe that each time there is a death, there is a birth. Early adolescents also have specific standards that are important to them, such as the idea that when something dies it should be buried.[8]

Fears of suffocation gradually replace mutilation anxiety. Consequently, concern about death includes a fear of being buried alive. Worries about pain and suffering also begin to appear as children think about their own death.

At approximately eleven years of age, children begin to use symbols of death in keeping with their growing ability to reason and think in abstract terms. Pictures drawn of death are realistic and may contain such objects as broken hearts, tears, or barren trees as symbols of the lifelessness, loneliness, and sadness that death leaves behind.[9]

Usually, early adolescents have gone beyond wondering what death is. At this point they are more caught up in relationship questions: Who will take care of Grandma now? What will happen to our family now that Dad has died? Concerned with practical issues, these children may wonder if the family's life-style will change, who will run the house, or who will make the money.[10]

In the preadolescent period, children reach a turning point in their development. Death becomes more abstract and spiritual. It is recognized as personal, universal, and real.[11] As they make the transition to a more adult view of death, early adolescents intellectually understand that death is final and irreversible. They are developing an acute sense of morality and may continue to consider death a punishment.

Children Twelve to Eighteen Years of Age; Adolescence

Twelve- to eighteen-year-olds share many adult concepts of death and cope with death in a similar manner. With well developed cognitive skills, adolescents intellectually understand that death is universal, inevitable, and irreversible.

As adolescents search for independence and meaning in life, they become very concerned with their bodies. They want to be attractive, loved, and accepted. Wanting to be different from their parents, they use their friends as measures of success or failure in family, school, or social life.

Because death destroys life and body, it is particularly threatening to adolescents. Death means that the beauty, handsomeness, strength, and capabilities of a person's body are lost forever. With puberty, adolescents watch their bodies change and mature. They may become aware of the natural progression of aging that makes death possible. Death, then, is seen as the natural enemy to this new self that is emerging.[12]

Adolescents are future oriented. This does not mean that they do not review the past or think about the present. They do, but their emphasis is on the future. Thoughts become philosophical. The adolescent asks, "Who am I?" "What am I going to do with my life?" "What about this thing called death?" "If a person grows up to die, then what is the sense of life?"

Death means that life can be interrupted and that goals may be destroyed or never reached. Adolescents often want to withdraw or deny a loss through death. The reminder of their own mortality may be too threatening or overwhelming. The thought of unfulfillment may fill them with despair or resentment. Their own mortality is kept in the distance, superseded by youth, plans, and the future.

In *Listening and Responding,* Davis says that adolescents are in the process of tumultuous change, most of which is completely out of their control.[13] Each person needs a certain degree of autonomy in life. When control is lost in one area, an individual is likely to compensate by asserting control in another. Denial or defiance of death may prompt some adolescents to challenge death by driving at excessive speed or experimenting with drugs.

Finally, some adolescents may reject funeral customs in their desire to avoid death. They do not want to make a public spectacle of their sorrow. They prefer to mourn in private or to sort out their feelings with friends.[14] An exception may be when their friends are mourning as well (for example, when a classmate or teacher dies).

If we can understand what children already think about death, we will be better equipped to discuss death with them. And by anticipating their fears, we can help them handle those fears, grow more comfortable with the concept of death, and be able to grieve.

3

How to Talk to Children about Death

EFORE DISCUSSING the concept of death with children, it is important to take time to reflect on how we feel about our own mortality. Children are inquisitive about all aspects of the life cycle, and we can answer their questions better if we have pondered them beforehand. If we are unaware of our own feelings about death, we will be unprepared to deal with those feelings when confronted by children's innocent questions.

Children are astute. They can often read our body language. If we are uncomfortable when we talk about death and have not dealt with these feelings appropriately, we may unknowingly communicate only that death is something to be feared or dreaded. Although we might be *saying* that death is a natural occurrence in life, nonverbally (through our tone of voice, our eyes, our body posture), we might be communicating fear. Mixed feelings about death are to be expected, but we must help children move toward an acceptance of death as part of the cycle of life.

How to Tell a Child a Loved One Has Died

Every situation involving death is different. Before discussing a death with a child, consider the following questions:
- What is the age and maturity level of the child?
- Does the child understand the meaning of the words *died* and *dead*?

- Has the child experienced a death prior to now (a family pet, a grandparent or parent, a classmate or teacher)?
- How was the child related to the deceased? How well did they know each other?
- What are the family's religious beliefs about death?
- What were the circumstances surrounding the death?
- What is the child's usual pattern of coping?

The answers to these questions provide basic information about the child's understanding of, and experience with, death. As discussed in the last chapter, children gradually develop a concept of death that is directly related to their age, but it is also affected by numerous other factors. The older or more mature child will have a more comprehensive understanding of death as will the child whose life has already been touched by death. In a situation in which the child and the deceased were emotionally close, the feelings of grief will be more intense than if they were not significantly attached.

The family's religious views also need to be considered. The child whose family believes in life after death might be comforted by the thought of Grandpa and Grandma being reunited in heaven with God. The circumstances surrounding the death must also be taken into account. A death situation involving a lingering illness is quite different from a case of suicide or murder.

Finally, the child's usual pattern of coping will impact how he or she will deal with the death. If children tend to cope with difficult situations by denying them, then they will probably do the same in a situation involving a death.

With the above information in mind, we are now ready to discuss the death with the child. The following suggestions are offered as guidelines, but remember that each situation is unique, and the child's reaction will be influenced by numerous factors.

Establish Rapport

Open the Lines of Communication

When you are ready to begin the discussion, find a quiet place where you can talk with the child and not be interrupted. In this initial conversation, provide only the basic information. State simply who has died, and what caused the death. If necessary, explain what the word *dead* means. Avoid overloading the child with detailed information. He or she will probably be overwhelmed and unable to hear details at this time. The goal is to open the lines for further communication so that the child will feel comfortable asking for additional information later.

Answer Truthfully

All children can understand the experience of death at some level, so their questions regarding death must be answered truthfully and in words they can understand. Inconsistent or incomplete answers may leave the child more unsettled than the truth itself.

If children sense that information is missing, their need to find a beginning, middle, and end to a story will lead them to fill in the blanks with their own answers. Often these imaginative answers will turn out to be far more disturbing than the truth itself. Children can be spared the terror of their imaginations if they are provided with truthful answers in a simple and direct manner.

When Andrew, an eight-year-old boy, was told that his mom died of a serious head injury from a car accident, he worried that she had been badly mutilated. Andrew knew she was dead, but the thought of his mom being disfigured really bothered him. When he saw her body in the coffin at the funeral home and peeked at the back of her head, he finally had a better idea of what had happened. When asked what he saw, Andrew said, "She had a cut, but it wasn't bad at all. My dad wouldn't tell me anything, and I thought it would be a lot worse." Because his questions weren't sufficiently answered, Andrew had to seek his own answers. And, as is often the case, he found that the truth wasn't as bad as his imagining.

Answer Only What Is Being Asked

When answering children's questions, make sure you understand what they are asking and provide only that information. Referring the children's questions back to them can clarify their specific concerns and help us know what is bothering them.

For example, if a child asks what will happen to Grandpa now that he has died, we might say, "What do you think will happen to Grandpa, Terri?" If she says something about his going to heaven to be with Grandma, then we can better understand what she is asking and can answer her appropriately. We will not respond with a detailed explanation of how the body will be buried in the ground and then eventually decompose. The child would likely walk away from that explanation, feeling confused and hurt because no one understood what she was trying to ask.

Encourage the Expression of Feelings

Communicate to children that it is ok to show their emotions. Let them know that even people who have similar feelings might each express them in different ways. Sharing our own feelings with children encourages them to express their feelings with us.

Children tend to look to their parents for guidance, and they will often model their behavior after them. For example, if Daddy is willing to share his feelings of sadness with Stevie and to let him see his tears, then Stevie will probably feel comfortable doing the same. If, on the other hand, Stevie never sees his daddy's tears, he might get the message that it's not ok for boys to cry. He might even think that Daddy didn't love the person who died as much as he did. If feelings are shared openly and honestly, both through words and actions, then miscommunication is much less likely.

Accept the Feelings and Reactions Expressed by the Children

Avoid telling children how they should or should not feel and how they should or should not act. Each child will respond to a death in his or her own way. We must recognize and respect this.

Although there are many common feelings and reactions to a death, the grieving process for each child will be a little different. We should not assume that because Kelsey expresses sadness at her father's death, Jason feels the same. He might feel deserted by his dad, and he may feel angry, thinking Dad somehow agreed to die. Both of these children's feelings are valid and need to be accepted and understood for what they are.

Avoid Euphemisms and Confusing Explanations of Death

When talking with children about death, avoid using euphemisms. Euphemisms are less direct words or phrases we use to keep from saying words we find distasteful. Avoid terms like *gone away, eternal rest, sleeping, passed on, lost, left us,* and *gone on a trip.* Instead, simple terms like *dead, stopped breathing,* or *wore out* can establish the fact that the body is no longer alive biologically.

We adults can put euphemisms into context and decipher their message. Children often cannot. These words do not mean the same to them as they do to us. Euphemisms tend to confuse rather than comfort.

For example, children who are told that their grandma is sleeping will wait for her to wake up as she always has in the past. They might also, after a while, resist going to bed at night, fearing that they, like Grandma, might not wake up.

Children who hear that their friends have lost their sister might think that this means she is lost as their little brother was lost at the department store last year. Then of course the sister will be found alive and well just as their brother was.

Finally, children who are told that their daddy has left them or gone on a trip might become confused and angry. The terms *left us* or *gone on a trip* imply a choice, causing children to wonder why their daddy would choose to leave them. Avoid making statements that will have to be retracted later. We want to lay a framework of truth to build upon as the child develops.

Integrate Personal Religious Beliefs into the Explanation

When discussing death with children, be careful to share only information that is consistent with your religious beliefs regarding the soul, heaven, and afterlife. Realize, too, that what is comforting to adults might be confusing, even frightening, to children.

For example, if you have not yet introduced the concepts of life after death and heaven and you tell Carmen that her father has gone there, don't be surprised if she asks how her daddy will get to heaven when his body has just been buried in the ground. If you tell her that her daddy is in heaven watching over her, this could produce more fear than comfort. Carmen will be left wondering if Daddy sees everything she does. Will Daddy see when she hits her brother or when she takes a cookie from the cookie jar?

When discussing personal religious beliefs with children, think about how they may interpret them. If we were to say to Kevin that God has taken his mommy to be with him, Kevin might become angry or disillusioned with God. He will wonder why a loving God would take his mommy when he needs her so much. If Kevin overhears someone saying that God takes the good to be with him in heaven, Kevin might worry that if he is good, he too will be taken.

Finally, if Kevin is told that his mommy was ready to die and be with God because she was hurting so bad, he might feel abandoned and become angry with his mother for choosing to leave him.

It is important to share with children only those religious beliefs that we sincerely hold to be true. If we share a concept we have reservations about, the children will almost certainly detect our hesitation and become confused.

For example, because we want to comfort Misty, we may tell her that Brandon will get a new bike in heaven, or Grandma will be able to bake her blueberry muffins there. Although Misty is hearing the words, she will sense the contradictory nonverbal cues. Not only will this leave her questioning our truthfulness, it will also confuse her developing beliefs.

Again, as we reflect on our own mortality, beliefs, and feelings about death, we can better help children with their questions.

4

Common Behaviors of Grieving Children

CHILDREN WHO HAVE EXPERIENCED the death of someone important to them may react in various ways. Some children will exhibit many of the following reactions; others will demonstrate only a few. Some reactions will occur right away; others may be delayed for some time.

Denial

- I can't believe it. She couldn't have died!

- My daddy didn't really die. He went away on a long trip. I know he'll come back!

Tony's mother had been sick for almost a year before her death. But because she had always come home after other stays in the hospital, Tony, age four, didn't believe it when he was told that his mother wasn't coming back this time.

It wasn't until his mother had been dead for almost six months that Tony began to realize she wasn't coming back. After attending his mother's wake and funeral and visiting his mother's grave a number of times, the message was becoming clear. And when Tony asked people "When is my mommy coming back?" they consistently told him she wasn't coming back.

Still Tony hoped for his mother's return for another few months. He couldn't imagine life without her. Denial provided periods of reprieve from his overwhelming sense of loss and abandonment.

Denial is not unusual. Death often comes as a surprise; and children, like adults, react in shock. If the information is too difficult to comprehend or accept, it is pushed away or denied for a while.

Often children will resume playing almost immediately upon hearing of the death. This does not mean they did not love the deceased or are not affected by the death. Rather, it is the children's way of dealing with the loss as they come to terms with it. Just as adults need to take a break from difficult situations, so do children.

Panic

- Mommy, are you going to die too?

- Who will take care of me?

- What is going to happen to me?

Children tend to be self-oriented and will often worry about how their needs will be met now that the structure of things has changed. This is particularly true for children whose parent has died. Often these children ask the surviving parent, "Who will take care of me when you die?"

At such a time, children need to know that we love them very much and that they will always be taken care of, either by us or by someone else they know and love. Let them know that you understand how scary it would be for them if you were to die too. But reassure them that you don't think you will die for a long, long time, and discuss who would take care of them in the unfortunate event that you were to die.

Anger

- How could Mommy die and leave me all alone?

- Why didn't the doctor save him?

- Why would God let my friend die?

Bereaved children often feel angry about the death of someone close. This anger may stem from a feeling of helplessness or loss of control. Usually children direct anger outwardly.

For example, a daughter may openly express her anger at her deceased father for leaving when she needed him most. This is particularly true when children perceive that the deceased had a

27

choice in his or her death. Children may also direct their anger at the doctor or at God, blaming them for not saving the loved one.

Indirectly, however, children might express their anger by acting out at school or at home, often set off by little things.

It is important to accept and understand this anger for what it is. Explore the children's anger with them, assuring them that it is ok to feel the way they do. Clarify any misconceptions they might have and then gently correct them. Communicate the importance of expressing anger openly. Try to help the children find appropriate ways of venting anger (punching a pillow, talking with a parent or friend, engaging in physical activity to burn off excess energy).

Guilt

- If only I hadn't yelled at him, then he'd still be alive.

- I shouldn't have said I hated him.

- It's my fault. I've been acting so horrible lately.

Mary, a thirteen-year-old, had had a stormy relationship with her father prior to his death in an industrial accident. Before he left for work on the day of his death, Mary and her dad had been involved in a huge fight. Mary said, "We were fighting about something really stupid. I wanted to go out with my friends, and he wouldn't let me. I told him I hated him and wished he wasn't my dad. And then he died. I feel so guilty."

Mary knew that her angry words did not cause her father's death, and yet at some level she felt responsible for the accident. She knew that she couldn't change the past, but she wished she would have done things differently. "If only I had told him that I loved him. I feel so bad that I yelled at him."

At times children may turn their anger inward and blame themselves for the death of their loved one, as Mary did. They might believe that something they said or thought or did somehow caused the death. Explore the children's feelings with them. Clarify any misconceptions they might have and explain the cause of death in terms they can understand. Emphasize that something in the body was not working right or that the death was accidental. Reassure the children that their words, thoughts, or actions did not and could not cause this to happen.

It may be difficult to convince children of their innocence if they firmly believe they were somehow responsible for the death, but keep reinforcing that an internal problem from illness or an accident caused the death.

Regression

The death of a loved one often causes significant changes in the children's routine. The security of their world is disrupted and they may be overwhelmed. Lacking the adult ability to cope, children may regress to earlier behaviors. For example, children who are potty trained may suddenly begin wetting their pants again. Children who have been developing their independence may become unsure of themselves. Children who have been in touch with reality may revert to the fantasies of earlier years.

Children need increased support at this time. They need to know they are loved and that their needs will be met. In order to restore some security to their world, follow their normal routine as closely as possible. Avoid any changes that increase stress and further disrupt their lives.

Bodily Distress and Anxiety

- I can't sleep.

- I'm not hungry. My stomach hurts.

- I feel sick like Johnny did when he was dying.

At times bereaved children may experience symptoms similar to those of the deceased prior to death. Explore these symptoms with them to determine the cause. It could be that they are seeking additional attention. Explain that although this is a difficult time for everyone, you will do your best to give them the attention they need. Reassure them that you love them very much just the way they are, and that you always will.

They may also experience bodily distress because they are confused about what causes death, and are frightened that they too might die. If this is the case, ask them what they know and think about death. Clarify, in terms they can understand, any misconceptions they might have. Reassure them that you will continue to take care of them.

If the death was the result of an illness, explain the difference between a chronic or terminal illness and a common one. If an accident was involved, explain that it was a very serious accident and that the person was hurt so badly that the body quit working. Reassure the children that you will continue to be careful and do all you can to avoid accidents.

Clinging or Replacement

- Please don't leave me, Mom. I don't want to stay with the babysitter.

- Grandpa, do you love me as much as Dad did?

Many children become tearful and clingy whenever they anticipate a separation. It is common for children who have experienced the death of someone close to be concerned that other people they love will also die. Explain to them that something in the deceased person's body was not working right, and that caused the death. Reassure them that you are healthy and do not anticipate dying for a very long time.

When you are going to be separated from the child, tell him or her where you are going, who you will be with, what you will be doing, and when you will be back. This information, if given in terms the child can understand, will help alleviate some anxiety.

Bereaved children might also try to replace the deceased by seeking the affection of another person. It is as if they are trying to find a substitute who will fill the void.

Tell the children that everyone will miss the deceased very much and that it will be difficult to live without that person. Reassure them that although no one will ever be able to take the place of the deceased, there are many people who love them and who will take care of them.

Preoccupation with the Deceased

- I remember how we used to. . . .

- Dad would have done it this way.

- This was always Mom's favorite place.

Bereaved children, like adults, may find themselves thinking about the deceased all the time. It is almost as if there were no escaping the memories. There are constant reminders wherever they look. These reminders may cause the children to experience unrelenting pain. In an attempt to find some relief from the overwhelming sadness, they may withdraw from the people and things that remind them of the deceased.

Reassure the children that this is normal and that you are all remembering the loved one who has died. Share your memories and talk about the feelings you are experiencing. Emphasize that running away from the situation will not make it go away.

Hyperactivity

Grieving children may become hyperactive, jumping from one activity to another without any purpose, searching aimlessly for something to do. These children may also talk or giggle incessantly as they attempt to deal with death.

Provide these children with structured activities that will help them focus. Acknowledge that this is a difficult time and you want to help them in whatever way you can as they struggle through it.

Shortened Attention Span

- I just can't seem to concentrate on my schoolwork anymore.
- It's as if he's off in his own little world these days.

Bereaved children, like adults, may have difficulty paying attention or concentrating for any length of time. Explain that this is normal and that in time the children will be able to focus better. Reassure them that you know it might be difficult to concentrate on their schoolwork and you do not expect them to do as well right now. Let the children's teachers know of the death, too, so that they will be able to understand and work with possible behavior changes.

Withdrawal

Grieving children may withdraw from the people they love because they are afraid these people will die as well. They may avoid getting to know new people because they fear being hurt again.

Explore these fears and concerns with the children. Reassure them that you love them very much and that you expect to live a long time. Acknowledge that there is always a possibility that someone will die sooner than expected, but being able to know and love the person is worth the risk. Emphasize again that running away from a situation will not make it go away. Help them see that by withdrawing from the people they love, they are cutting themselves off from love and support at a time when they desperately need it.

Assumption of Mannerisms of the Deceased

- I can fix things just like my daddy.
- Don't I sound like my mom?

At times bereaved children may assume certain mannerisms of the deceased and begin acting or talking like that person. Assure the children that you all loved the person who died and you will miss that person very much. Remind the children that they are special and that you love them just the way they are. Emphasize that although they may in fact have some characteristics of the deceased (the same knack with tools, a similar voice or laugh, the same smile), this is not what makes you love them. Each child is special in his or her own way. It is this uniqueness that you love.

Idealization of the Deceased

- My grandpa was the best in the whole world!
- Nobody could do that better than my mom.
- My brother was good at everything he ever did.

Children often remember only the good things about the person who has died. While it is certainly comforting to remember these points, it is not healthy for children to fantasize that the deceased person was perfect.

Although we shouldn't force children to dwell on unpleasant memories, we should discourage the denial of such memories. If children idealize the deceased, they may have unrealistic expectations of other people in comparison. Emphasize that no one, not even the deceased, is or was perfect; but we can love them anyway.

Repressed Feelings Expressed Years Later

In some cases bereaved children may be unable to grieve the loss at the time of the death. Very young children may have difficulty understanding the significance of the death. Other children might not have the support they need. As a result, they may deny the death because they don't have the coping skills to effectively grieve.

If children do not deal with the death and express their feelings, at some point in the future something will trigger those feelings, and they will be confronted with the grief they had earlier repressed.

Because children grieve in many different ways, we need to be sensitive to our children's behavior as they struggle to accept the death of someone they love. Identify the behavior and accept it for what it is. Do all you can to understand their feelings and reactions. Then try to clear up misconceptions and give whatever reassurances you can.

5

Tasks
of Grieving

I N THE BOOK *Good Grief: Helping Groups of Children When a Friend Dies*, Sandra Fox says that for grieving children to make their grief "good grief" they must accomplish three tasks: 1) understanding, 2) grieving, and 3) commemorating.[1] The age and personality of the child, as well as the cause of the death, influence how bereaved children accomplish these tasks.

Understanding

Understanding the death means that the children know the deceased is no longer alive and will never again be a part of their day-to-day lives. To achieve this task, children need access to honest information in terms they can understand.

Begin with a simple explanation so that the children are not overloaded with information they are not yet ready for. This initial explanation should include the fact of the death, a clear statement about what the word *dead* means, some information about the cause of death, and permission to express both feelings and questions.[2]

Children will likely think about this initial explanation and then seek out additional information as they are ready. Provide them with enough explanation of what is happening so they won't have too many gaps in the story which need to be filled by their imagination. If children sense that we are holding back information or misrepresenting the truth, they will make their own assumptions based on their knowledge of the situation.

Grieving; Feeling the Feelings

Grieving means working through the various feelings that are a part of mourning. Although adults and children mourn in similar, predictable ways, the specific content and process of that mourning will vary according to the individual, the developmental level, and the situation.[3]

Various formal rituals can help children channel their grief appropriately. While these observances are often geared to the adult's expression of grief, don't forget to take the children's needs into consideration.

Although adults will often make the final decisions about the children's participation in these events, even very young children can be encouraged to talk about what is happening and what they would like to do. Tell the children what will be happening over the next few days (the reviewal or wake, the funeral, the burial, the memorial service). Explain the rituals in terms they can understand, letting the children know that these are ways we can say good-bye and show our respect to the person who has died. Given a clear description of what will happen and a choice about whether or not to participate in these events, children usually talk freely about what they would like to do.

The family may choose to schedule a private viewing outside of the public visiting time. This will ensure that children can, if they choose, see and touch the body in the presence of people whom they love and trust. It is often helpful to have the funeral director available during this time to answer the children's questions and discuss any concerns they might have. This will help the parents know what their children are thinking while taking the pressure off the parents at a time when they may be overwhelmed by emotion and unable to respond adequately to their children's questions.

Ideally, each child will be allowed, and encouraged, to participate at whatever level he or she feels comfortable. Some children will wish to be included in all of the formal rituals, while others will choose to attend only some of them. Some may choose to view the body while others will avoid seeing it. Some children will want to be involved in the funeral service and may share a special poem or reading while others may choose to place a gift in the casket.

Whatever the children decide, encourage them to participate only as much or as little as they choose. Children must not feel forced into doing something that isn't comfortable just because others are doing it. Offer options to the children. Understanding adults could stay with those children who choose not to participate in the formal grieving rituals. If children do attend the funeral, make sure there are enough familiar adults on hand to respond to their needs and concerns. These adults must also be available to leave the service with the children if they should become restless or disruptive.

Finally, acknowledge that each child's grieving will be an individual process. Just as the relationship between the deceased and the child was unique, so too is the sense of loss. For some bereaved children, the deceased will have been a very special part of their lives. For others, the relationship may have been much less significant. Each child will, however, have feelings and behaviors that express his or her grief. Make sure that the children know it is OK to feel whatever they are feeling and that they will be accepted wherever they are in the grief process.

Commemorating

To commemorate means to honor or keep alive the memory of someone or something. Commemorating the life of the deceased can range from informal remembering to a more formal marking of the death with some type of ceremony or observance.[4] Commemoration gives children an opportunity to affirm the value of the life of that person.

If you decide to have a formal observance, include the bereaved children in the planning if they wish to be, but attendance at any formal memorial service should be voluntary. Give children permission to be involved or not be involved, assuring them that you will respect their decisions.

Different decisions will be appropriate for each child. For example, the child who was close to the deceased will likely choose to be involved in the planning of a commemorative ceremony and may even elect to share something written or chosen to remember the person. The child who barely knew the person, on the other hand, may not even choose to attend.

Commemoration can also be informal. In many cases children may choose to do something tangible to remind them of the deceased. For example, many children select as memorials trees, shrubs, and flowers that bloom and grow annually. Jeremy may want to plant some rose bushes like the ones his grandfather had.

A trust fund may be established in memory of the deceased with the money being donated to a particular cause. Jennifer may want to give money to the American Cancer Society because she saw how much the organization helped her mom while she was sick. Whatever the method of commemoration, it should represent the wishes of the dead person's family and friends and help in the grief process.

Eventually, the formal or informal commemoration so important at the time of the death will become less of a focus. Life goes on, as it must.[5] In *The Dead Bird* when M. W. Brown writes about young children who find a dead bird, she says they bury it, mark the grave, and bring fresh flowers. They understand, grieve, and commemorate—until they forget.[6]

Outcome of Successful Grieving

William J. Worden, in *Grief Counseling and Grief Therapy: A Handbook for the Mental Health Practitioner,* says that successful grieving helps a person to: 1) accept the reality of the loss, 2) experience the pain of grief, 3) adjust to an environment in which the deceased is missing, and 4) withdraw emotional energy and reinvest it in another relationship.[7]

Young children need to meet these challenges on a child's level and a child's timetable. But healthy grief requires all four components. Children will, for example, believe us when we say that the deceased will no longer be part of their day-to-day lives except in their memories. They will express their feelings and accept a new person performing some of the deceased person's roles or functions. They will also be able to view the world as a place where they can love and trust.[8]

6

How to Help Grieving Children

THE THREE TASKS OF GRIEVING described in chapter 5 form the foundation for the material in this chapter about how we can help children grieve. Information about the tasks is supplemented by further insights and practical suggestions.

Be Aware of Personal Feelings

Before attempting to help bereaved children, take time to reflect on your own feelings related to the death of the deceased as well as your feelings regarding the fact that you will someday die. Your ability to deal with the reality of the situation will set an example for the children's acceptance or denial of the death.

When we are in touch with our own feelings (sadness, loss, regret), we will be better able to help bereaved children cope with theirs. Then we can work together with the children toward a healthy resolution of grief.

Recognize That Each Child's Level of Understanding Is Different

Remember that each child's understanding will vary according to such factors as age and developmental level. Provide the children with information and responses appropriate for their age level. Then build on this information as their understanding gradually develops.

Recognize That Each Child Will Grieve Differently

Although many people may be having similar feelings, the grief process is an individual experience. How children will grieve the death is influenced both by the responses of those close to them and by their relationship with the deceased.

When Brian, age twelve, learned that his father had died of unknown causes, he wasn't sure how to feel. Brian's father had not lived at home for almost six years, and their relationship prior to that was unstable. The father tended to be violent after he had been drinking, and Brian remembered being beaten frequently as a child.

Therefore, when Brian heard about his father's death, part of him was sad, but another part was comforted by the fact that his father could no longer hurt him. Confused by these mixed emotions, Brian needed over a year of counseling before he was able to resolve them.

Encourage Questions

When someone dies, children usually want to know what has happened and what will happen now, and they have a right to this information. Tell them honestly what has occurred and explain, when necessary, what the word *dead* means. Let the children know that you want to help them through this and that you are willing to talk with them about all aspects of the death, including their feelings about it.

Reassure the children that you will do your best to answer their questions, but don't be afraid to say, "I don't know." If they sense that you are giving them honest information and not withholding the truth, then they will feel comfortable talking with you about the situation. Usually they will ask a few questions and then go away to think about what you have said. When they are ready for more information, they will come back with additional questions.

If at any time you cannot deal with the children's questions (when you are physically or emotionally exhausted, for example), tell them why you can't explain now. Then tell them when you will be able to talk with them. If you do not do this, the children might think you are avoiding the issue. They may begin to question your honesty and your willingness to talk with them.

Encourage the Expression of Feelings

Let children know that it is ok to show their emotions. Sharing your feelings with children is one of the most effective means of encouraging them to express their feelings with you. Children tend to look to their parents for guidance and will often model their behavior after Mom and Dad.

Help children realize that although everyone might have similar feelings, they will each express them differently. For example, Nicky may think that his mommy isn't saddened by Daddy's death because he has never seen her crying. What he does not know is that she cries herself to sleep at night, but she doesn't want Nicky to see her tears. Or maybe Grandma seems to be very angry with Nicky for something that he did. But in fact, she is angry with the doctor for failing to save her only son. Nicky needs to understand his grandmother's feelings.

If adults share their feelings openly and honestly, children are much more likely to feel comfortable expressing their own feelings. Fewer problems develop when children don't have to guess how others are feeling and grieving.

Encourage Participation in Events Following the Death

Spend some time preparing children for the events that will occur during the first few days following the death. Often what is most distressing for bereaved children is not knowing what will be happening and how they fit into the picture. Outlining the next few days following a death could save children from unnecessary anxiety during what is already a very difficult time.

As described in chapter 5, tell the children about the events that will be taking place (reviewal or wake, funeral, burial). Explain that these rituals provide us with a way to say good-bye to the deceased. Answer any questions they might have about the rituals. Give the children permission to choose the extent of their participation. Emphasize that they will not be forced to do anything that does not feel comfortable to them.

Help the Child to Commemorate the Life of the Deceased

It is often beneficial to help children find a meaningful way to commemorate the life of the deceased (also described in chapter

5). Share your favorite memories of the person with them and invite them to do the same with you. It may be possible to offer the children a possession that holds special meaning for them. For example, Tyler would probably be grateful for one of the fishing poles he and his grandpa used to share.

Ask the children how they would like to remember the loved one. Help them find ways to do this. If, for example, Erin and her grandmother used to play under a particular tree at Grandma's house, then maybe Erin would like to plant a similar tree at home in her own backyard. Assisting children with such a memorial will help facilitate a healthy resolution of their grief.

Try to Maintain a Sense of Normalcy

Grieving children often find their world in turmoil. To restore some semblance of security, try to follow the children's normal routine as closely as possible. This will bring some structure and stability to an environment that seems completely out of control.

If you are overwhelmed and unable to adequately care for the children yourself, consider having someone familiar to them come to your home to help you during this difficult time. Then the children can still be near you and feel a part of what is happening, but you can be relieved of the responsibility for their care. If the children are sent away, they may feel that their grief is unimportant because they are being excluded from sharing in the family's grief.

In the first few months following the death, try to avoid making any drastic changes, such as a move, unless the change is absolutely necessary. These changes may seem positive to us, but change often increases stress for children.

Use Available Resources

When grieving the death of a loved one, we may feel completely overwhelmed, barely able to meet our own needs, much less provide adequately for the needs of the children. Communicate your feelings to those around you and seek the assistance that you need.

Initially, it is important to have help with the details of the funeral and wake. You may also have various offers to help with routine household chores (cooking, cleaning, laundry). Don't be afraid to accept these offers.

As time goes on, however, you may need a friend who not only recognizes the importance of simply being there but who is also willing to listen attentively as you share the feelings you are experiencing. Whatever the case, remember that just as adults may need assistance in their grief work, children may, too.

A number of resources are available to help bereaved children through a healthy grieving process. The school, church, or local hospital may offer a children's loss support group. Children, although initially somewhat reluctant to attend these groups, will usually benefit by going to one.

When children get together with other bereaved children, they become aware that they are not alone in their grief; other children have also experienced the death of someone close. They realize that the feelings they have are normal and that it is ok to ask questions about death as they attempt to gain a greater understanding of it. They not only learn the value of expressing their feelings, but they also explore methods of coping with those feelings appropriately and effectively.

Local bookstores and libraries have numerous books that can prepare us for our interactions with grieving children (see "For Further Reading," p. 76). Some are designed to be read together with the children. Others are directed toward the adult. Still others are available for the children to read. Often a children's bookstore can be most helpful in finding current books on this topic.

Finally, counselors who specialize in the area of grief and bereavement can help both you and your child. While not all children will require one-on-one counseling, there are cases when it does become necessary. The feelings of grief are initially intense. If they are addressed and dealt with appropriately, however, the intensity will gradually ease. When the feelings remain intense for an extended period of time, additional intervention may be required.

If your children do not seem to be getting over the death (as evidenced by the continuing intensity of their feelings and reactions to the death), or if you have any questions or concerns, do not hesitate to call a counselor. Even if a counseling session reveals that your children are in fact grieving the death as would normally be expected, at least you can rest easier. You will know that they are doing the best they can in a difficult situation.

7

Death Education

CHILDREN CAN LEARN to accept death as a natural occurrence in life, even though neither they nor we are free from negative feelings about it. It is our responsibility as adults to introduce the concept at an early age in an objective and nonthreatening manner. By doing this, we will help them develop a healthy understanding of death. Because of their own inability to confront issues related to death, many parents do not even try to educate their children on the subject. They leave the job to other people: teachers, health-care providers, religious education instructors. This is less than ideal, however, because children's exposure to death may not wait until they have been given proper death education.

All too often the concept of death will not be introduced until there is a crisis situation, such as the death of a parent or grandparent. At that point, family members are usually emotionally overwhelmed and cannot adequately explain what has happened. In the ideal situation, children will have had the opportunity to explore the concept of death and to ask questions about it before they are confronted with the death of a person (or a pet) with whom they have a significant emotional attachment.

Children are inquisitive. As they grow and develop, they are constantly exploring their environment in an attempt to figure out how everything works and fits together. Just as children wonder about life, they also wonder about death. They should be taught that death is a part of life, just as being born, eating, drinking, sleeping, talking, crying, and laughing are a part of life.

Teaching children about death and confronting our own feelings and beliefs regarding death can be difficult. May your efforts be rewarded as you undertake the challenge of death education in your home, your school, and your church.

In the Home

Take Advantage of Teachable Moments

Learn to watch for teachable moments to introduce and discuss the concept of death with your children, preferably before a death occurs within the family. The death of a person or a pet with whom you and your child are not close provides an excellent opportunity to explore the subject in a calm manner at a time when you are not emotionally upset.

Nature itself provides a multitude of circumstances that can assist us in this teaching process: 1) a dead bird lying on the sidewalk; 2) a dead fish washed up on the shore of the lake; 3) worms found shriveled up on the sidewalk after a rainstorm; and 4) a dead animal on the side of the road. These common examples are excellent opportunities to introduce the subject of death.

The changing seasons also illustrate the natural cycle of life and death. Every spring we observe the trees budding and the flowers blooming. In the fall we see the leaves turn color and fall to the ground, and, after the first frost, the flowers shrivel and die. Over time, the dead leaves and flowers decompose, eventually becoming a part of the soil and providing nourishment for the new life we will observe the following spring.

The death of a family pet or a distant relative can also provide a good lesson if it is discussed openly and honestly. At this time we can talk about the various rituals of grieving and encourage the children to participate in them at whatever level feels comfortable.

Children are also exposed to death through the media. Be sure to talk to them about this to avoid unnecessary confusion. For example, a character may die on one television show and then appear alive again, either in a repeat episode or on an entirely different program. Television can, in some cases, reinforce a young child's belief that death is reversible. Obviously this will need to be clarified.

By taking advantage of teachable moments, we can help prepare children for the personal losses that they will inevitably experience.

A number of storybooks and fairytales can also help in the process of death education. Some are listed in the section "For Further Reading," p. 76. Ideally these books will have been read with the children before a death occurs within the family. Books can be used effectively to supplement or reinforce the information gleaned from a teachable moment because the children's curiosity about death will already have been aroused.

Share Basic Religious Beliefs About Death

When teaching children about death, it is important that we share with them our religious beliefs concerning it. We may choose to talk about the concept of resurrection and being with God in heaven.

When discussing our religious beliefs with children, we must be sure to share only what we truly believe. If we are unsure of something (whether we sleep for a while or go to heaven directly after death, for example), then we should admit we don't know. Children can see through inconsistencies. Be honest about what you know and what you believe, based on your faith.

Provide Basic Information About the Causes of Death

When telling children about a death, discuss with them what caused the death. If, for example, the person died from an illness, clarify that it was a very serious illness, not one children often experience, like the flu, a cold, or a sore throat. If the death was caused by an accident, clarify that the body was injured so badly that it could no longer function properly and so it stopped working completely.

Provide for Positive Separation Experiences

One of the earliest childhood fears is separation from their care-givers. Young children are not able to differentiate between a short, temporary absence and a long, possibly permanent one. Any separation can produce anxiety for them.

We can alleviate some of this fear by structuring positive separation experiences into the children's lives. Begin with very short time periods, say ten minutes, and then gradually lengthen the time that you are away. Leave the children in the care of someone they know and trust. Explain in terms they can understand where you are going and when you will be back.

For example, before you leave, you might say, "Grandma has come to take care of you while Mommy goes to a meeting at church. You can play outside for a while, and then Grandma will feed you lunch and get you ready for your nap. Then, when you wake up, I will be back, and Grandma will have gone home."

After you return home, spend some time with your children to see how their time went without you. Discuss any concerns that they might have. If you are consistent and follow through on what you say (be home after their nap if that is when you said you would be home), then children will become familiar with these separations. Their separation anxiety will decrease. This in turn will help prepare them for the more significant separations that they will inevitably experience later on.

In the School

Take Advantage of Teachable Moments

School is a place where children are encouraged to learn and ask questions about things they don't know or understand. Obviously, this will include the concept of death.

Many of the teachable moments encountered in the home are also available to teachers. Teachers can improvise with these moments, and then supplement them with further, perhaps more formal, education in the classroom. Take advantage of the naturally occurring deaths within the environment (dead animals, how winter kills many plants), as well as the unexpected ones (the death of a school employee or a fellow student), as you take on the challenge of death education.

Integrate the Concept of Death into the Academic Curriculum

Death education can be structured into the formal academic curriculum, including existing classes (such as science, health, or religion), or it can be taught as a separate course.

The staff who are teaching these courses should at least: 1) have some specialized training in the area of death education; 2) be aware of, and comfortable with, their own issues of mortality; and 3) demonstrate the ability to discuss death openly and honestly without conveying negative messages (verbally or nonverbally).

Some schools may choose to have a classroom pet, such as a gerbil or goldfish. If it dies, as such pets often do, the children will have a timely opportunity to plan a burial and possibly a service of some type.

In a science course, children can experience nature's life cycle firsthand by planting, nurturing, and harvesting a small garden. In a health class, they may learn how the human body works and discuss certain things which are and are not good for it. For example, they may discuss the benefits of proper nutrition and exercise, and the harmful effects of such things as excessive use of drugs and alcohol. They may also differentiate between common, chronic, and life-threatening illnesses, and talk about what happens when the body is seriously injured. Some classes even visit a local funeral home to learn more about what happens to the body after it dies.

Finally, in a religion course, children have an opportunity to discuss the spiritual aspect of death, such as heaven and new life with God, free from pain and sadness.

In the Church

Take Advantage of the Teachable Moments

Children tend to be curious in most environments, the church included. Teachable moments are also available here. The children may see a crucifix in the church and wonder about its significance, or they may hear the priest or pastor request prayer for a person close to death. They may even read a notice of a death or a funeral in the church bulletin and ask about that. We can take advantage of these moments to build on what the children already know about death, which may or may not include the spiritual aspect of it.

Integrate the Concept of Death into Religious Education Classes

Children can also be instructed about death in their regular religious education classes. The Easter season, for example, provides a good opportunity to talk about life after death, about Jesus' resurrection and ours. Discussion of the deaths of prophets and martyrs provide other openings for death education in the church setting.

Share Your Faith as Faith, Not Fact

When discussing our religious beliefs with children, it is important that we clarify what we know as fact and what we believe based on our faith. The facts about death are actually rather limited. We know that the body ceases to function for any number of reasons, and the person is no longer able to breathe, eat, drink, sleep, talk, laugh, feel, touch, move, or do any other of the things that people who are living can do. The body becomes lifeless, like an empty shell, and is buried in a cemetery or cremated. Although we can visit the remains of the deceased, the life of the person, often called the soul or the spirit, is no longer present.

Christian faith, not medical science, teaches us that, because of Jesus Christ's death and resurrection, after our death, we will be reunited in heaven with God and all the other faithful people who have died before us. Beyond this basic doctrine, we enter into speculation. We do not know what or where heaven is or what it is like, other than that it is full of light, joy, and peace. We do not know how the spirit or soul of the departed person gets there or whether or not the deceased can see and hear us in our day-to-day lives. Children, being children, however, want to know these things.

Since children tend to think in concrete terms, they have difficulty even imagining something as abstract as the soul or spirit, God, and heaven. As a result, they will often fill in the blanks created by the answers we provide based on our faith. For example, heaven is often imagined as a place in the sky filled with people who are healthy and happy and doing their favorite things. How do they get there? Well—on a cloud, of course!

It is best not to contradict the children's images. We ourselves do not know what heaven is like, and so there is no point in taking away something that the children find comforting simply because we may imagine it to be a bit different.

Simply share your faith openly and honestly. Then encourage the children to explore and challenge their faith as they attempt to integrate it with their own beliefs.

Avoid Portraying God as a Taker

When discussing religious beliefs with children, think about how our beliefs might be misinterpreted. For example, if we say to Sarah, "God has taken your daddy to be with him in heaven," she might become angry and disillusioned with a God who would take away her dad. Rather than telling children that God takes people, we can say that we don't know why tragedies happen and then gently reassure them that God is waiting with open arms to receive loved ones when they die.

Avoid Saying, "It Was God's Will."

When children overhear adults saying that it was God's will for a person to die, they may become confused, particularly if they have been taught that God is a kind and loving being who watches over them like a parent. Parents would not deliberately hurt their child. So why would God do such a thing? They might think that he must know that people are hurt deeply by the death of a loved one, so why would he will somebody to die? The next thought could be that God might not be such a kind and loving being after all.

Rather than suggesting that death is God's will, we can explain it as a part of the mystery of life. The mystery of life and death as we know it contains numerous opportunities that challenge us to grow in our faith. We certainly do not seek out or ask for these difficulties. Yet once we encounter them, we can choose how we will handle them. Difficulties can be a source of empowerment, or they can consume and destroy us. The choice is ours.

8

When a Child Is Dying

THE NEXT THREE CHAPTERS provide guidance for a situation we all hope we never have to face: helping dying children. Such a topic is appropriate for this book because these children are also grieving children. They are grieving the loss of all the people, places, and things they love, and they are grieving the loss of their own lives. As a pediatric nurse, I have worked extensively with children who have had some type of cancer or immune disorder, and I have cared for a number of them in the terminal stages of their disease.

All seriously ill children, regardless of age and how much they are told about their disease and prognosis, are aware of the gravity of their situation. For some, this awareness is a basic understanding; for others, it goes much deeper. This awareness develops gradually over a period of time. Prior to their illness, these children probably entertained the innocent notion that everything could somehow be made all better.

The diagnosis of a life-threatening illness, however, brings with it some harsh realities. Mom and Dad can't always take away the hurt and make everything ok. Some things, such as cancer, penetrate even a parent's protective shield. Doctors, with their advanced knowledge, technology, and treatments, cannot cure all of life's diseases. And no matter how good the children might try to be, their cooperative behavior will not prevent the outcome of their disease.

The initial hospitalization for diagnosis, and subsequent visits for treatment, may overwhelm the children, their parents, and their families. Numerous tests and procedures (blood draws, bone marrows, spinal taps, scans, X-rays) are often unpleasant and uncomfortable.

Parents anxiously await results that confirm the dreaded diagnosis of cancer or some other fatal disease. Children themselves, even if unaware of the significance of all that is happening, know that something serious or unusual is taking place.

Changes in Daily Routine

The children find themselves in an environment that is often unfamiliar and frightening. Their daily routine is interrupted for various tests and procedures. Meals may be delayed or held, with diet subject to change (regular, clear liquid, full liquid).

Naps and playtime are squeezed in as schedule and time allow. Sleep may be disturbed to take a temperature or give medication. Numerous physicians and other health-care professionals repeatedly examine the children. Nurses care for them in ways parents usually do (changing diapers, bathing, feeding).

Siblings stay at home with relatives or neighbors and may not be able to visit on a regular basis. The children cannot attend school and may no longer have daily contact with their friends. Their world has been turned upside down. The security provided by the normal daily routine is gone. Away from home, in another world, they are forced to adapt to a new, often chaotic routine.

Hospitalization Versus Clinic Visits

Children rapidly learn that the hospital is not like the clinic they go to for a sore throat, earache, or any other of the typical childhood ailments. They are not allowed to go home at night, and they are more apt to be separated from their parents, for example, when they go to surgery.

Because they often need intravenous medication, the children soon acquire an I.V. pump and pole. They are told their medications will help them get better, yet, to the children, those medications do not appear to be working very well. In the past when they took medicine, such as an antibiotic for an ear infection or high fever, they soon felt better. These new medications, however, often make

51

them feel even sicker for a period of time. For example, nausea and vomiting are frequent side effects of chemotherapy.

Finally, children quickly realize that people in the hospital mean business. Although children may be offered some choices, they do not have the option to refuse required treatment or care. For example, the nurse may ask patients if they want to take their medications with juice or water but will not ask whether or not they want to take the medications. The nurse may ask if they want their blood drawn in their room or in the treatment room, but no one will ask if they want to have blood drawn.

Changes in Parental Behavior and Attitude

The parents of dying children tend to be emotionally overwrought and tense. Their faces are often drawn and tight, stained by many tears. They may appear frightened and upset. They do not have all of the answers; instead, they have many questions of their own. Hushed conversations in the hall with physicians or on the telephone with family and friends imply there is some secret.

Parents, rather than protecting the children, are now demanding that they do unpleasant things. Children are urged to cooperate for uncomfortable tests and procedures. They are forced to take medications that often do not taste good.

At the same time, parents may become overindulgent, showering the children with gifts and giving them whatever they want. Parents' expectations may change as well. They may accept behaviors not normally tolerated: acting out, hitting, kicking, screaming.

Finally, parents who would usually be at work may now be at the hospital. Mothers may be sleeping in the children's hospital rooms while fathers stay home at night with the other children.

Changes in Body Image

Medications have various side effects which can alter the children's physical appearance: weight loss or weight gain, loss of hair, jaundice (yellowness of skin and whites of eyes), tendency to bruise easily, paleness, and/or mouth sores.

The children may also need various tubes: a central I.V., a feeding tube, a nasogastric tube, and/or a foley catheter. With these kinds of changes, the children know something is seriously wrong.

Changes in the Condition of Hospital Friends

Hospitalized children still need to play, and in many cases are allowed to participate in floor activities coordinated by child life specialists or volunteers. Through play, children can experiment with what is happening to try to gain some understanding of it.

Often during these play activities, the children will socialize with other children on the floor. In many cases they form friendships and regularly compare notes about all aspects of their illness. As a result, when one of them takes a turn for the worse, the other children soon realize that something is not quite right. Maybe they aren't seeing their friend at the clinic or in the hospital anymore. Or maybe, when they saw the child last, he or she looked very, very sick and wasn't able to play. Or maybe they overheard the nurses or their parents talking about their friend.

Children are aware of everything that is going on in their environment. If they are not told what has occurred, they will form their own conclusions based on what they have seen and heard. If and when they conclude that their friend has died, the seriousness of their own illness will take on an added dimension. Now they begin to wonder about the possibility of their own death.

Changes in Their Own Condition

When children achieve a remission from their disease, they may be lulled into a false sense of security as life reverts to some semblance of what it used to be. In many situations, however, this illusion is shattered by a relapse. The daily routine must again accommodate illness. Usually, they have to return to the hospital.

As parents again begin acting as they did at the time of diagnosis and additional physical changes take place, the children become even more aware that something serious or unusual is happening.

If the disease does not respond to treatment or complications of the treatments threaten normal functioning, these are more clues that point to a very serious condition. Parents confer with physicians to discuss options. Ideally the children will be involved in these discussions, but even if they are not, they are probably still aware of the situation.

Children can add up the clues and figure out that they are not getting better, that they may be dying. Physicians may present a last-ditch treatment plan that could have life-threatening side effects. A move to the intensive care unit surrounds them with machines that sustain their life and monitor their condition.

On the other hand, the focus of care may change from cure to comfort. Unnecessary treatments and procedures will be considerably reduced and comfort measures employed. Parents may choose to take their children home and possibly attempt to fulfill a child's final wish (a trip to Disney World, a chance to meet a famous athlete).

As the children move closer to death, their physical condition may change. They may tire more easily, so they become less active. They may lose control of various bodily functions (bowel and bladder, movement and sensation) and exhibit little or no interest in food or drink. All of these changes let them know they are dying.

Dying children know something is terribly wrong. As they observe changes around them—outside and inside—they need to be free to talk about what's happening to them.

Stages of Dying

Elisabeth Kübler-Ross's work with terminally ill people led her to propose five stages of dying: denial, anger, bargaining, depression, and acceptance.[1] Although these are usually applied to adults, dying children may also move through the five stages. Very young children may not understand that they are dying, but older ones gradually realize what is happening. They, like adults, do not necessarily move through the five stages in the order just presented; many exhibit two or three stages at the same time, and they may regress to a stage they had previously worked through.

The first stage, denial, is experienced by almost all dying people, not only when they are told of their serious illness but also later from time to time. Denial functions as a buffer, allowing patients to collect themselves and eventually find less drastic coping mechanisms.

When denial can no longer be maintained, it is replaced by feelings of anger, rage, envy, and resentment. The terminally ill person asks, "Why me?" Their anger lashes out in all directions and can be projected onto almost anything in their environment at random.

The third stage, bargaining, can be helpful although only for brief periods of time. If they have been unable to face the sad facts in the first period and have been angry at people and God in the second phase, maybe they can succeed in making some sort of agreement to postpone the inevitable, they reason.

When terminally ill adults or children can no longer deny their illness, their numbness, anger, and bargaining will soon be replaced with a sense of loss and depression. Dying people are in the process of losing everything and everybody they love. If we allow them to express their sorrow, they will find final acceptance much easier.

Kübler-Ross says that if people have had enough time and have been given help in working through the other stages, most will reach a stage of acceptance during which they are neither depressed nor angry about their fate.[2] It is as if the pain is gone, the struggle is over, and the person rests before the long journey ahead.

These stages of dying have often been applied to the grief process. Upon learning of the death of a loved one, many of us can probably remember the initial shock, followed later by anger, depression, and at some point, acceptance. But remember that adults and children don't move through acceptance of death or grief in a predictable manner. People often experience several emotions at the same time (anger and sadness) and feel a sense of peace one day only to find their sense of loss unresolved the next. Grief is an individual process, influenced by a variety of factors. In moving toward the ultimate acceptance of a death, many people feel that for every three steps forward, there is at least one backward.

9

Concerns of Dying Children and Their Parents

CHILDREN WHO ARE DYING will have many concerns, and we can help them if we can anticipate some of their fears, worries, and questions.

Fear of Abandonment or Isolation

Children who are in the terminal stage of their illnesses will often worry about being abandoned, not only by the nurses, physicians, and other health-care personnel, but also by their families and friends. They may find that the doctors are not stopping in to see them as regularly or that their favorite nurse has not dropped in for a surprise visit lately.

Their friends may not have come around for a while despite the fact that they have been invited numerous times. Even family members may become too busy to spend time talking and playing with the children. Consequently, the children may begin to fear that they will be alone at the time of death.

Children may sense that others feel uncomfortable with the fact that they are dying. Some might even go so far as to attempt to hide various symptoms in order to ensure that they will not be abandoned.

In both of the following examples the child senses the discomfort of a family member or friend and alters his or her behavior in an attempt to protect others from the pain and sadness associated with impending death.

Adam, a ten-year-old in the terminal stage of leukemia, noticed that his mom would start crying and make an excuse to leave the room whenever he asked what was going to happen to him. He had overheard the doctors talking to her and knew that he was not going to get better. Adam wanted desperately to discuss this with his mom, but he soon realized that it was too difficult for her. Because he needed his mother with him, he decided not to mention his concerns about his impending death. Adam hoped that if he didn't talk about it, his mother would continue to stay with him.

Sixteen-year-old Emily, terminally ill with cancer, noticed that her friends didn't seem to want to visit anymore. And when they did come, they barely said anything. They seemed especially uncomfortable around her when she wasn't up and dressed.

As a result, whenever her friends were coming to visit, Emily made an extra effort to look the best she could. No matter how uncomfortable she was feeling, she would get up, get dressed, put on her wig, and even apply some makeup. Not wanting to be alone, she was willing to be uncomfortable to make her friends feel more comfortable. By doing this, Emily hoped to avoid being abandoned by her friends.

Terminally ill children may also feel isolated from the world and the people in it. Not only are people visiting less frequently, when they do come they don't talk with the children as they used to.

In the past, visitors would relate stories about what was happening in their lives, what was going on at school, who won the baseball game, what they were planning to wear to the dance and what movie they wanted to see. As the disease is progressing, they don't seem to know what to talk about. It is almost as if people are afraid to discuss the events of everyday life because they know the children won't be alive to enjoy these activities much longer, and it hurts to think of a future without them.

Even though reminders of a lost future may sadden dying children, it probably hurts even more to be excluded from the present world. They may not have much time left, but they are still alive. So, if they wish to continue to participate in certain activities, try to accommodate them. Certainly the children will face limitations, but usually the pleasure of being involved will more than compensate.

Consider Jody, for example. For as long as she could remember, she had been going to watch her older brother play in various sports. Although her physical condition now prevented her from attending the games, she continued to be interested in how her brother played and who won the game.

As time passed, however, Jody noticed that her brother didn't talk about the games unless she initiated the conversation. When asked how this made her feel, she said she was hurt and angry. Beginning to wonder if her brother even loved her anymore, she felt that maybe he was just waiting for her to die.

Her brother, on the other hand, said he didn't think Jody would care about his games anymore. They seemed insignificant compared to the fact that she was dying. He realized later, however, after talking with her about this, that the games were something special she shared with him. By continuing to take an interest in her brother's ball games, despite the fact that she could no longer attend, Jody felt she could still be a part of his life.

Fear of Retribution

Human nature seems to want to find someone or something to blame when a situation goes wrong. Because children tend to engage in magical thinking, seriously ill children often believe that something they said, thought, or did somehow caused all of their troubles.

Because it is difficult to understand and accept that the cancer just happened for some unexplained reason, the children often review their past to determine what, if anything, could be responsible.

Twelve-year-old Joey firmly believed that he became sick with cancer because he had stolen candy from a store several years before. It didn't matter to him that he had been reprimanded by his parents and had returned the candy. Somehow that was not enough. In Joey's mind, God was punishing him for his behavior.

While discussing the situation, Joey said that he imagined God to be a loving and forgiving God, yet, clearly, he did not believe this in his heart because he continued to maintain that he was being punished for his past mistake. Joey needed to blame someone, so he blamed himself. It had to be his fault. Why else would he be dying? Why else would he have gotten cancer? This must be how God was punishing him.

Missy, a six-year-old with recurrent lymphoma, was sure that she had relapsed because she hadn't taken all of her medication. After all, her mom and the nurses had told her repeatedly, "If you take all of your medicine like a good girl, you'll get well again."

Missy had never told anyone about the pill she had spit out when the nurse was not looking. Surely it was because she had not taken that one pill that the cancer had come back and she was now dying.

Fifteen-year-old Tony was dying because, as he said, "I didn't want to get better bad enough." His family believed that if you want something badly enough and pray about it, then you will get it. It followed then, that if Tony had wanted to get better badly enough, he would have recovered. If he had prayed about it, he wouldn't be dying.

Fear of Dying and Death

Dying children often have fears associated with the dying process and with death itself. For example, what will it be like? Will they be in pain? Will they lose control of their bodily functions? Will they be conscious, aware of what is happening? Will it be scary? Who, if anyone, will be with them? What will happen after death? What will happen to their bodies? How will they get to heaven? Will they know anyone?

Mike, a fifteen-year-old who was first diagnosed with cancer at the age of twelve, underwent treatment and had been in remission for almost a year when the cancer recurred. A new treatment plan was devised at that time, but the response was disappointing.

Mike and his parents soon realized that the cancer was not going to be cured. Together they elected to continue treatment for as long as it was helping to keep the disease in check, hoping to buy Mike some quality time. They were, however, realistic about the expected outcome and discussed it openly.

The cancer ultimately spread to Mike's lungs, causing increasing breathing difficulties. Aggressive therapy was stopped, and Mike chose to return home to die. He was anxious about *how* he would die; he said he particularly feared suffocation. Mike was assured that everything possible would be done to keep him comfortable with medications and oxygen.

As his condition deteriorated, however, Mike became more anxious and decided to return to the hospital because he felt most comfortable there. When he arrived, he appeared distressed, but after a short time, he visibly relaxed. Within several hours, he died a quiet and peaceful death, surrounded by his family and friends.

Seventeen-year-old Amy, diagnosed with cancer two years earlier, was now in the terminal stage of the disease. Although she appeared to accept the fact of her impending death, she complained angrily about the indignities that would accompany it.

In the last days before her death, Amy lost the ability to move from the waist down as well as the ability to control her bowel and bladder. Although she had always prided herself on being able to take care of her own needs, Amy feared that even this would gradually become impossible.

As her care became increasingly difficult, Amy saw herself as a burden on her mom. At one point she said, "It's bad enough that I have to go through this, Mom, but it's even worse that you do too." She apologized for the situation as if somehow she were responsible for it.

The hospital staff did their best to respect Amy's continuing need for privacy and dignity, striving to let her do what she could for herself. Ultimately Amy learned to work with her limitations and was able to return home for about a month before she died peacefully in her sleep.

Peter, barely four years of age, wondered aloud what it would be like in heaven. His startled mother, not knowing what else to say, replied, "I don't know, Peter. What do you think it will be like?"

Peter thought about it for a while and then looked at his mother and said, "There won't be any more pokes, and I'll see my friends with cancer again. But we won't be sick anymore!"

Four-year-old Kathy told her mom not to worry about her after she died. Knowing that her grandfather was in heaven, Kathy was sure he would be waiting to greet her and to help take care of her.

The families and friends of dying children share many of the concerns of the children themselves. Understanding these fears can help defuse them.

Parental Fear of Abandonment or Isolation

Just as dying children fear that they may be abandoned, family members and even friends may fear they will be left alone. The subject of death, especially when it involves a child, often makes people uncomfortable. When a loved one is dying, the family and friends need to talk about it. Unfortunately, they may discover that people they thought they could turn to are not able to help.

Rather than face their own fears and concerns, these potential supporters may avoid the uncomfortable and quit calling or visiting. If they do continue to visit, they may deny the impending death, change the subject, or leave whenever anyone talks about death. The family and friends are then faced with having to find new support in the midst of what is already a difficult situation.

Fear of Failure in the Role of Parent and Protector

Parents of dying children often wonder if they are in some way responsible for the situation. They may think, "If only I had taken her to the doctor sooner, maybe the treatment would have worked better, maybe the outcome would have been different. Why did I assume she just had the flu?" or "Maybe he got sick because we live in the city with all the pollution and smog. Why did I ever agree to take this new job and move?"

Parents, like their children, want to know the whys, hows, and whats of all that is taking place. It seems easier, somehow, if we can understand why or know where to place blame than to accept that cancer just happened for some unexplained reason.

Parents may also feel they have failed their children in some way. After all, parents are supposed to be able to protect their children from all of the bad things in life. Does their child's cancer diagnosis mean that they have failed in their parental responsibilities?

How do parents know if they will be able to make the right decisions regarding treatment and care? How can they be sure that the benefits of treatment will outweigh the complications and side effects? Who is to say that their child won't be one of the few who survive because of the new drug the doctors are offering?

Will they know if and when they have done enough for their child? Will there come a time when discontinuing aggressive therapy is the right thing to do? What if they get new information that makes them believe they made a wrong decision earlier? Does that mean they have failed as parents?

Fear of Coping with a Child's Pain and Death

Parents often wonder how they will be able to endure watching their child suffer and die. A sense of helplessness is common. They may feel inadequate to comfort their child. At the same time, however, they may feel guilty for thinking of their own pain when they consider the pain their child is facing. What kind of parents are they if they can't handle the situation?

There may come a time when parents look to death as a blessing because it will mean an end to their child's pain and suffering. This, too, however, may overwhelm them with guilt. How do you live with yourself when you pray for the death of your child? Will other people be able to understand these feelings? Will they accept you and your feelings?

Dying children may have many concerns: fears of abandonment, isolation, and retribution; questions about the process of dying and the moment of death itself, and perhaps uncertainty about what comes after death. The parents and families of dying children will share some of those same concerns, but children and parents must freely communicate all of their feelings and fears.

10

Providing Care for Dying Children

W HENEVER POSSIBLE, try to provide consistency in the arrangement of caregivers for children who are dying. The children are at a point where they need to conserve energy for the activities of their choice (reading a story with Mom, visiting with a special friend). It could be stressful and energy wasting if caregivers are not familiar with the children, their families, their situations, and their routines. Caregivers can provide dying children with a special understanding.

How to Help Dying Children

If you are the parent of or a caregiver for a dying child, you are in a position to offer the child unique help. Your role is vital.

Emphasize That the Children Have Done Nothing Wrong

Dying children need to feel loved. They must understand that this illness is not their fault. Explore their ideas about why this is happening, and try to correct any misconceptions they might have.

If children are firmly convinced that they are somehow responsible for the illness because of something they said, thought, or did, you may be unable to convince them otherwise. But continue to express your unconditional love and let them know you will be there for them no matter what. Gently try to dissuade them from believing they are somehow to blame, but don't force this, or they may shut you out and refuse to talk with you about their fears.

Be Honest in Your Communication with the Children

Most children don't ask a question without expecting some type of answer. So if dying children ask a question, it is our responsibility to provide an answer. Take care, however, to avoid burdening them with excess information. Answer only what is being asked, using terminology they can understand.

Children are not always direct. They may ask questions or make statements that indirectly indicate their understanding or awareness of the situation. Consider the following examples.

Allison, a fourteen-year-old girl with lymphoma, asked me, "What happens if this chemo doesn't work?" I had been caring for Allison on a regular basis for more than six months, and she knew this was the last treatment available to her. As I explored the question, she later rephrased it by saying, "I know there are a limited number of treatment options available. And I also know that I have used all but the one I am taking right now. So, if this one doesn't work, then am I going to die?"

Mark, an eleven-year-old boy with endstage leukemia, asked if he could do his Christmas shopping early that year. Christmas was his favorite holiday, and he wanted to be sure that he was ready for it. Although it was only October, his parents obliged. Mark spent an afternoon at the mall selecting his gifts. When he got home, he wrapped and labeled the gifts, then put them in his closet. Within a week, his condition began to worsen. He died several days later.

Other questions include:

Who will get my toys?

Do you think my friends will remember me?

I wonder if Grandpa (who died several years earlier) will recognize me without my hair.

All of these questions reflect sincere thought and deserve honest answers. When talking honestly with these children, we also need to be aware of nonverbal body language.

Facilitate Communication and the
Expression of Feelings

Gently encourage honest communication between the child, family, and caregivers; but do not force communication. For example, if Eric has trouble asking his physician questions, he may ask you, the caretaker, to do it for him. Or if Eric senses that his parents are uncomfortable talking with him about his fears and concerns, he may look to you, a trusted caregiver, to listen. Eric might also ask you to talk to his parents about their discomfort and let them know how much he needs to share his thoughts with them.

Some parents use denial as a means of coping with the situation. If we are caregivers, we have to accept the fact that we cannot force parents to deal with their children the way we want them to. Some people can never let go of their denial. They hang on to it regardless of the circumstances. A caregiver's primary responsibility is to the children, to meet *their* needs. In the next two examples, parents used a form of denial to protect either themselves or their children.

Chris, a sixteen-year-old boy, had been diagnosed with leukemia at age twelve. For many years, his mother, a single parent, had used alcohol to cope. Chris and his family lived out of town, and his mother would often bring him to the hospital for treatments and then go back home until Chris was ready to leave again. On rare occasions, if he was very ill, she would stay in town at a local hotel. Even then, however, she spent little time at the hospital with her son. When she was in town, she would often call the hospital about two in the morning (after the bars had closed) to see how her son was doing.

Chris accepted his mother's behavior, and though he knew she loved him, he also knew that she couldn't face the situation or offer him much comfort or support. Over the years Chris became very close to several of the nurses and one of the doctors.

When it became apparent that he was dying, Chris tried to talk with his mom, but she was too uncomfortable to listen. Chris realized that if he wanted support, he would again have to look outside the family. He knew that his mother was distressed at the thought of being with him when he died.

On the night before Chris's death, his mom said she wanted to go to a movie if he thought he'd be OK. He told her to go. After she left, his condition deteriorated. We asked Chris if he would like us to try to get a message to his mother. He said no, asking instead that we call the nurses and doctor he had grown close to. Within hours after they arrived, Chris died, surrounded by the people who had loved and supported him throughout much of his illness.

When his mother returned to the hospital, several hours after her son's death, she was able to go in and spend some time saying good-bye to Chris. She said, "If only I had known he was so sick, I never would have gone to the movie."

The caregivers knew how difficult it had been for Chris's mother to face both the illness and the inevitable moment of death, and they assured her that Chris had not been alone and that he died comfortably. In his own way, Chris had chosen to protect his mother from various aspects of his illness and ultimately from the moment of his death.

Rebecca, who had recently turned seven, was transferred from another hospital to receive an experimental treatment which was not available anywhere else. When she was diagnosed with bone cancer two years before, her parents told her she had a bone disease but said nothing about cancer. In her parents' minds, saying that people had cancer was the equivalent of saying that they were going to die. They believed that if they could keep Rebecca from hearing the word *cancer*, somehow they could prevent her from realizing how sick she was.

What the parents did not realize, however, was that Rebecca knew what was going on. Although she didn't hear her parents say the word *cancer*, she did overhear it from others. And sensitive to her parents' body language, she could tell that something serious was happening. The changes in her physical condition and the need for numerous extended hospitalizations gave further clues.

As desperately as her parents wanted to protect her from the truth, they could not. Instead, they gave Rebecca a very clear message: It is not ok to talk about the cancer. Rebecca was forced to turn to others for information and support.

In giving care to dying children, encourage them to express their feelings. The most effective way to do this is by example. Some parents feel they need to be strong for their child and try to hide their feelings. Others think their child is too young to understand what is happening.

In either case we, as caregivers, can help the situation by sharing with the child, in the presence of the parents, how we are feeling. For example, we might say, "It hurts me to see you so sick, Jared.

I wish that I could make you better, but I can't. I can see that you are sad, and I want to help you with that. Would you like to talk about it?"

By doing this, we show that we understand the seriousness of the situation and acknowledge that the child has feelings and thoughts related to it. By asking him to share his thoughts with us, we are further opening the lines of communication. Ideally, the family will then be able to express their feelings and to talk about them at a comfortable level.

Keep the Children Comfortable

Dying children will often have fears about how they will die and if they will be in pain. It is important to talk about these fears and let the children know that although we are not sure exactly how they will die, we will do everything we can to keep them as comfortable as possible.

Caregivers need to work with physicians and nurses to ensure that the children are receiving the most effective medications for controlling their pain.

Explore alternative methods of pain control as well, such as distraction techniques, guided imagery, meditation, music therapy, and gentle massage. By keeping children as pain-free as possible, we alleviate some of the fear and anxiety about their impending death.

Determine Goals

Take time to sit and talk with the children to find out if they have any goals that they would like to reach. A child may, for example, wish to take a trip to Disney World or meet a childhood idol, such as a famous actor. It could be something simple, such as attending the school class picnic or visiting with grandparents who will arrive soon from out of town. Whatever the case, determine what, if any, goals the children might have and then do your best to help them achieve those goals.

Explore the Concept of Heaven (When Appropriate)

Discuss with the children and their families what their beliefs are about what happens when a person dies. If they believe in life after death and the concept of heaven, explore with the children what they think heaven will be like. Not only will this ease some of their anxiety, but it will also provide them with something to move toward.

If, for example, Zachary views heaven as a happy place where there is no more pain and where people who have died are reunited with God, then he will be less fearful. He may envision a loved one, perhaps a grandparent, who awaits him in heaven with God.

Give the Children Permission to Die

At times children may worry about how painful their death will be for family and friends. Let them know that it will indeed be very difficult for us after they have died, but at the same time, assure them that their needs are most important now. For example, we might say, "I am sad, Lisa, and I will miss you very, very much because I love you so much. But I will remember you always in my heart and cherish the many memories that I have." Or "It hurts me to see you struggling so hard. You've been fighting this disease and beating it for a long time, but now it's time to rest. Now it's time to let go."

How to Help Family Members and Friends

Offer Assistance and Follow Through

Family members and friends are usually grateful to people who offer assistance during this difficult period. Although they might not need anything at the time the offer is made, they find comfort in knowing who they can call if something comes up. But if you *do* make an offer to help, be sure to follow through with it.

If, for example, you say that you will take care of a younger sibling for an afternoon, make sure to do exactly that. Family members and friends are vulnerable. They need to have people they can rely on. If they can't think of anything specific that they need help with at the time, then call periodically to see how they are doing, and again offer assistance. This shows your genuine concern and lets them know that you have not forgotten about them.

Be Specific When Offering to Help

Some people have difficulty asking for or accepting assistance. They may be accustomed to taking care of things by themselves, or they may feel as if they have taken up too much of your time already.

In this situation, it often works best to be very specific when offering to help. Rather than saying, "Let me know if there is anything I can do to help," and then waiting for them to call, we can say something like, "I'd like to make a casserole and bring it over. Would tomorrow evening be OK?" Or "I'm going to the grocery store this afternoon. What can I pick up for you?"

Families and friends of children who have died have said that the following things were helpful to them:

1. Assistance with household chores: laundry, light housekeeping, meal preparation, grocery shopping;
2. Transportation: to the hospital, the store, a sibling's sports event;
3. Assistance with other children: babysitting them either in their home or yours for an afternoon or evening; taking siblings to the park, the zoo, a movie, any activity that can give them a break from the situation;
4. Assistance with the child who is dying: sitting with the dying child so the parents can rest, have an evening out, spend time with their other children, attend to business matters;
5. Visiting or calling to see how the child and family are doing;
6. *Listening* when they need to talk.

Provide Support, Not Answers

Family members have undoubtedly been asking themselves over and over why this is happening and what, if anything, they might have done to cause it. Acknowledge that it is very difficult to understand and may be even impossible to accept. Avoid blaming them for the child's illness or burdening them with your own theories about why this might have happened.

For example, it might be helpful to say, "I'm so sorry. I just don't know what to say. It's difficult to understand why this is all happening." Never say things like, "If you had taken him to the doctor sooner, maybe they could have saved him," or "You never should have let him eat so much junk food. It's full of chemical additives."

Affirm Them as Loving Parents
Capable of Making Good Decisions

Parents of dying children are in an extremely difficult situation—one they would never have elected to be in. Encourage them; they are doing the best they can under the circumstances. Affirm them as good and loving parents and let them know they have not failed in their role of parent and protector. Cancer is a disease that can happen to anyone; it is not something children can be protected against.

Once cancer touches a family numerous decisions must be made. Parents may become overwhelmed, wondering how they will ever be able to make the right decisions. If they ask, help them gather the information necessary to make the best decisions for their child. Remind them that there are no right or wrong decisions. Emphasize that they are doing the best they can with the information available at the time.

Accept the Parents Where They Are

It is very difficult for parents to watch their child suffer and die, and to deal with the overwhelming sense of powerlessness. Commend them for ways in which they have comforted their child in the past. Offer suggestions about how they can continue to comfort their child now (holding her hand, stroking her head, snuggling in bed, reading a favorite story, listening to a soothing tape, taking a ride in the wagon, inviting a friend for a short visit, preparing a favorite dish).

Help the parents see how well they have handled many difficult situations since their child's diagnosis. Gently reassure them that somehow they will manage to get through this. Remind them to take care of themselves, too, so that they will have the strength to meet their child's needs. Encourage them to reach out for the help they need.

Finally, accept the parents where they are. Taking care to remain nonjudgmental, encourage them to share their thoughts and feelings. At this time the family needs love and support more than anything else. It would be highly inappropriate for caregivers to second guess the parents' decisions.

Every situation is unique, and each family will make the decisions they feel are best for their child. People don't choose to have cancer enter their lives. Yet, when it does, they do the best they can in a difficult situation. Although they did not choose the diagnosis, they can choose how they will live with it, and in some cases, how they will die with it. We must support and accept these choices, knowing that they required much thought and anguish.

Conclusion

W E ALL KNOW that death is a part of the mystery of life, but we never know exactly how or when it will enter our lives. Children today may reach adulthood without ever experiencing the death of someone close to them. Unless adequately prepared, they will have difficulty coping with a death when it occurs. It is our responsibility to prepare children for the inevitable losses in life by introducing the concept of death to them at an early age, using the teachable moments available.

Children are naturally inquisitive about death, just as they are about life. It makes sense, then, that we seek to educate them. Children are eager to learn. If we convey the message that it is not ok to talk about death, they will simply find another source for their information. Rather than attempting to hide death from children, we should discuss it openly, honestly, and naturally.

Children obviously do not understand death the same way adults do. The concept develops gradually over time as children grow, learn, and experience life. When teaching them about death, we must tailor the information to their individual needs.

If a child approached you today with a question about death, would he or she feel comfortable exploring the concept with you or would that child need to go to someone else? It is my hope that you are now better prepared to help educate the children you encounter about death and that you feel more comfortable answering their questions and helping them grieve.

A Tribute to Molly

MOLLY was a very special young lady. I had the privilege of knowing her for almost three years. During that time Molly became much more than a patient to me; she became my friend. I first met Molly on the day of her diagnosis, and I was with her at the moment of her death. It was a profound experience.

One of the first things I realized about Molly was that she was not a complainer. No matter how much she was hurting or how miserable she felt, she rarely complained. She took everything in stride. I was continually amazed at her courage and strength.

The disease took so much from Molly. She lost the security of her health, the routine of day-to-day life, and the childhood innocence that believes Mom and Dad can somehow make everything all better. She lost her hair, her leg, a lung, and ultimately her life. Yet through it all she remained strong, even until the moment of death. Molly taught me that no matter how difficult a situation might seem, there is always something to be gained from it if only we have the courage to look for and find it.

About a week before her death, I asked Molly how she wanted to be remembered. She said, "As a fighter. I never gave up." I asked her if she understood that when she became a hospice patient she was still not giving up, she said, "Yes," and then she looked me right in the eye and said, almost angrily, "Why? Don't you think I'm still fighting?" I replied, "Oh, Molly. Yes! I know you are. You've always amazed me by your ability to bounce back from everything."

I remember how quickly Molly was up and getting about following her amputation. Pain had always been an issue for Molly, and yet it never stopped her. She continually picked herself up and moved forward. Her last autumn, after a little over a year of remission, Molly returned to the hospital. The disease had spread to her lung. When I talked to Molly about this, she said, "I know if it came back this once, it'll probably come back again, and I'll have to go through this (thoracotomy; incision of the chest wall) all over again." The thought of that really scared her, and yet several months later she came back again for another thoracotomy. At that time it was necessary to remove the lung. Molly was faced with what was probably the most difficult decision of her life: Did she want to begin treatment again, or did she feel it was time to stop?

Molly knew that even with treatment she had almost no chance of buying herself any additional time. And she knew that more treatment would mean time in the hospital, away from home, and that she would be very sick. She made the decision not to begin treatment again. She chose, rather, to return home to be with her family. She wanted to live and enjoy the time that was left to her—and enjoy it she did. On the Thursday before her death, she went shopping with her mom (one of her favorite things to do). On Friday, she went to a movie with her family. Even as she was dying, Molly was living fully. Molly was Molly.

As difficult as some moments of her final days were, Molly continued to be concerned about others. She wasn't quite ready to die, and she needed to continue to give to others as she always had. Her family reassured her that she didn't have to be strong for them, that she could rest. But it wasn't her time yet; Molly wasn't ready. She needed to fight for life just a little bit longer.

By Monday night Molly was ready to die. She had fought a long, hard battle with cancer; and now she was ready for it to be over. She looked at each of us, and her final words were: "I love you, Dad. I love you, Jason. I love you, Mom. And I love you, Theresa." With that, Molly turned her head and died. It could not have been more beautiful. Molly was now at peace. She would struggle no more, and there would be no more pain.

I'll miss you, Molly—good-bye.

Notes

Chapter 1

1. A. Davis, *Listening and Responding* (St. Louis, Toronto: The C. V. Mosby Company, 1984), 238-60.
2. Robert Kastenbaum, "The Child's Understanding of Death: How Does It Develop?" in *Explaining Death to Children* ed. E. Grollman, (Boston: Beacon Press, 1967), 89-108.
3. Kastenbaum, *Explaining Death*, 89–108.
4. Kastenbaum, *Explaining Death*, 89–108.
5. Dan Schaefer and Christine Lyons, *How Do We Tell the Children?* (New York: Newmarket Press, 1986).
6. Davis, *Listening and Responding*, 238–60.
7. Kastenbaum, *Explaining Death*, 89–108.
8. Davis, 238–60.
9. Schaefer and Lyons, *How Do We Tell the Children?*
10. John Schowalter, "The Child's Reaction to His Own Terminal Illness" in *Loss and Grief: Psychological Management in Medical Practice*, eds. B. Schoenberg, et al. (New York: Columbia University Press, 1970), 51-69.
11. D. Adams and E. Deveau, *Coping with Childhood Cancer: Where Do We Go from Here?* (Reston, Virginia: Reston Publishing Company, Inc., 1984), 137–98.
12. Schowalter, *The Child's Reaction*, 51–69.
13. Schaefer and Lyons.

Chapter 2

1. Robert Kastenbaum, "The Child's Understanding of Death: How Does It Develop?" in *Explaining Death to Children*, ed. E. Grollman (Boston: Beacon Press, 1967), 89-108.

74

2. A. Davis, *Listening and Responding* (St. Louis, Toronto: The C. V. Mosby Company, 1984), 238–60.
3. John Schowalter, "The Child's Reaction to His Own Terminal Illness" in *Loss and Grief: Psychological Management in Medical Practice*, eds. B. Schoenberg, et al. (New York: Columbia University Press, 1970), 51-69.
4. Davis, *Listening and Responding*, 238–60.
5. Kastenbaum, *Explaining Death*, 89–108.
6. Davis, 238–60.
7. D. Adams and E. Deveau, *Coping with Childhood Cancer: Where Do We Go from Here?* (Reston, Virginia: Reston Publishing Company, Inc., 1984), 137–98.
8. Schowalter, *Loss and Grief*, 51–69.
9. Adams and Deveau, *Coping with Childhood Cancer*, 137–98.
10. Schowalter, 51–69.
11. Adams and Deveau, 137–98.
12. Schowalter, 51–69.
13. Davis, 238–60.
14. Adams and Deveau, 137–98.

Chapter 5

1. S. Fox, *Good Grief: Helping Groups of Children When a Friend Dies* (Boston: The New England Association for the Education of Young Children, 1985), 7–38.
2. H. Dunton, "The Child's Concept of Grief" in *Loss and Grief: Psychological Management in Medical Practice*, eds. B. Schoenberg, et al. (New York: Columbia University Press, 1970), 355–61.
3. Dunton, *Loss and Grief*, 355–61.
4. Dunton, *Loss and Grief*, 355–61.
5. Fox, *Good Grief*, 7–38.
6. M. W. Brown, *The Dead Bird* (New York: Dell Publishing Company, Inc., 1979).
7. William J. Worden, *Grief Counseling and Grief Therapy* (New York: Springer Publishing Company, 1982), 11–16.
8. Fox, *Good Grief*, 7–38.

Chapter 8

1. Elisabeth Kübler-Ross, *On Death and Dying* (New York: The Macmillan Company, 1969).
2. Kübler-Ross.

For Further Reading

Books for the Educator

Dodd, Robert V. *Helping Children Cope with Death.* Scottdale, Pennsylvania: Herald Press, 1984.

Kübler-Ross, Elisabeth. *On Children and Death.* New York: Macmillan Publishing Company, 1983.

Rudolph, Marguerita. *Should the Children Know?* New York: Schocken Books, 1978.

Schaefer, Dan and Lyons, Christine. *How Do We Tell the Children?* New York: Newmarket Press, 1986.

Wolfelt, A. *Helping Children Cope with Grief.* Muncie, Indiana: Accelerated Development Inc., 1983.

Books to Read with Children

Brown, M. W. *The Dead Bird.* New York: Dell Publishing Company, Inc., 1979.

Grollman, Earl A. *Talking about Death: A Dialogue Between Parent and Child.* Boston: Beacon Press, 1970.

Johnson, Joy and Johnson, Marvin. *Tell Me, Papa.* Grand Neck, New York: Centering Corporation, 1978.

Mellonie, B. and Ingpen, R. *Lifetimes.* New York, New York: Bantam Books, Inc., 1983.

Sanford, Doris. *It Must Hurt A Lot.* Portland, Oregon: Multnomah Press, 1986.

Stein, Sara B. *About Dying.* New York: Walker and Company, 1974.

Death of a Friend

Blackburn, L. B. *Timothy Duck*. Omaha, Nebraska: Centering Corporation, 1987.

Cohn, J. *I Had a Friend Named Peter*. New York: William Morrow and Company, Inc., 1987.

Smith, D. B. *A Taste of Blackberries*. New York: Harper and Row, Publishers, 1973.

Varley, S. *Badger's Parting Gifts*. New York: Lothrop, Lee and Shepard Books, 1984.

Death of a Parent

Hammond, J. M. *When My Dad Died*. Ann Arbor, Michigan: Cranbrook Publishing, 1981.

Hammond, J. M. *When My Mommy Died*. Ann Arbor, Michigan: Cranbrook Publishing, 1980.

Papenbrock, P. L. and Voss, R. F. *Children's Grief*. Redmond, Washington: Medic Publishing Company, 1988.

Death of a Sibling

Johnson, Joy and Johnson, Marvin *Where's Jess?* Omaha, Nebraska: Centering Corporation, 1982.

LaTour, K. *For Those Who Live*. Dallas, Texas: Kathy LaTour, 1983.

Richter, E. *Losing Someone You Love*. New York: G. P. Putnam's Sons, 1986.

Scherago, M. *Sibling Grief*. Redmond, Washington: Medic Publishing Company, 1987.

Sims, A. *Am I Still a Sister?* Albuquerque, New Mexico: Big A & Company, 1986.

Death of a Child

Miles, M. *The Grief of Parents When a Child Dies*. Oak Brook, Illinois: The Compassionate Friends, Inc., 1978.

Osgood, J. (Editor), *Meditations for Bereaved Parents*. Sunriver, Oregon: Gilgal Publications, 1983.

Schatz, W. *Healing a Father's Grief*. Redmond, Washington: Medic Publishing Company, 1984.

Schiff, H. S. *The Bereaved Parent*. New York: Crown Publishers, 1977.

Teen Bereavement

Gravelle, K. and Haskins, C. *Teenagers Face to Face with Bereavement*. Englewood Cliffs, New Jersey: Julian Messner, 1989.

For Further Reading

General

Adams, D. and Deveau E. *Coping With Childhood Cancer: Where Do We Go from Here?* Reston, Virginia: Reston Publishing Company, 1984.

Bluebond-Langner, Myra. *The Private Worlds of Dying Children.* Princeton, New Jersey: Princeton University Press, 1978.

Crase, Darrel and Crase, Dixie. "Helping Children Understand Death." *Young Children* (Nov. 1978): 21–25.

Davis, A. *Listening and Responding.* St. Louis, Toronto: The C. V. Mosby Company, 1984.

Dunton, H. "The Child's Concept of Grief" in *Loss and Grief: Psychological Management in Medical Practice,* edited by B. Schoenberg, A. Carr, D. Peretz, and A. Kutscher. New York: Columbia University Press, 1970.

Fox, S. *Good Grief: Helping Groups of Children When a Friend Dies.* Boston: The New England Association for the Education of Young Children, 1985.

Fredlund, D. "The Remaining Child." In *Home Care for the Dying Child,* edited by I. Martinson. New York: Appleton-Century-Crofts, 1976.

Furman, E. "Helping Children Cope with Grief." *Young Children* (May 1978): 25–32.

Glicken, M. "The Child's View of Death." *Journal of Marriage and Family Counseling* 4, no. 2 (April 1978): 65–71.

Kastenbaum, Robert. "The Child's Understanding of Death: How Does It Develop?" In *Explaining Death to Children,* edited by E. Grollman. Boston: Beacon Press, 1967.

Kopp, R. *When Someone You Love Is Dying.* Grand Rapids, Michigan: Zondervan Publishing House, 1980.

Krupnick, J. "Bereavement during Childhood and Adolescence." In *Bereavement: Reactions, Consequences, and Care,* edited by M. Green, M. Osterweis, and F. Solomon. Washington, D.C.: National Academy Press, 1984.

O'Connor, Nancy. *Letting Go with Love: The Grieving Process.* Apache Junction, Arizona: La Mariposa Press, 1984.

Rofes, E., ed. *The Kid's Book about Death and Dying.* Boston: Little, Brown, and Company, 1985.

Schowalter, J. "The Child's Reaction to His Own Terminal Illness." In *Loss and Grief: Psychological Management in Medical Practice,* edited by B. Schoenberg, A. Carr, D. Peretz, and A. Kutscher. New York: Columbia University Press, 1970.

Sharapan, H. *Talking with Young Children about Death.* Booklet produced in Pittsburg, Pennsylvania: Family Communications, 1979.

Sheer, B. "Help for Parents in a Difficult Job—Broaching the Subject of Death." *The American Journal of Maternal Child Nursing* (Sept.–Oct. 1977): 320–23.

Stein, Sara B. *About Dying.* New York: Walker and Company, 1974.

Wass, Hannebre, and Corr, Charles A., eds. *Childhood and Death*. Washington, D.C.: Hemisphere Publishing Corporation, 1984.

———. *Helping Children Cope with Death: Guidelines and Resources*, Second Edition. Washington, D.C.: Hemisphere Publishing Corporation, 1984.

Westberg, Granger E. *Good Grief*. Philadelphia: Fortress Press, 1962, 1971.

Worden, William J. *Grief Counseling and Grief Therapy*. New York: Springer Publishing Company, 1982.